BITTERMAN'S

CRAFT SALT

COOKING

BITTERMAN'S

CRAFT SALT

COOKING

The Single Ingredient That Transforms All Your Favorite Foods and Recipes

MARK BITTERMAN

RECIPES BY ANDREW SCHLOSS AND MARK BITTERMAN
PHOTOGRAPHY BY CLARE BARBOZA AND MARK BITTERMAN

**Andrews McMeel
Publishing**®

a division of Andrews McMeel Universal

TO MY FATHER,
HOWARD

CONTENTS

THE FOOD THAT TIME FORGOT

I awake early, an hour before the sun came up, eager to explore the salt farm. The air is warm on my skin, humid but fresh. Barefoot, I take the narrow path through the marsh grasses toward the salt ponds, through the cordgrass, flowering salicornia, and sea lavender. Salt crystals crunch under my feet as I pick my way along the rough wooden planks that cross the ponds. I stop in the middle, and the still waters around me mirror the golden fire of dawn reaching up through a purple sky, silhouetting the scattered volcanoes to the east and along the border of El Salvador to the south. Behind me, to the west, birds squawk like pterodactyls from the shadows of the mangrove forest, and the faint roar of the ocean fills up the space beyond. I kneel, sift my fingers through the brine, and touch the glistening crystals to my lips. The flavor is unlike anything on earth; this is craft salt.

Salt is a food that traces its roots back to the horizon where mankind meets nature. Over the millennia, across virtually every culture and locale, everyone who could make salt did make salt. It was never easy. Water had to be evaporated using the sun or fire from seas or salt springs, or raw salt rocks had to be broken and pulled by brute force from the earth. Environments like salt marshes had to be protected, and resources like wood had to be conserved. It took great ingenuity and skill, honed over centuries to a fine craft, to achieve salt making that was reliable and sustainable. Salt is one of the most varied, locally rooted, ingeniously produced, and distinctive foods on earth.

Our planet is home to many hundreds of craft salts, each a perfect, authentic reflection of its native ecology, economy, and culinary tradition. But in order to use them, you don't need access to every one. For practical use, there are only seven categories of salt, which all of the hundreds of varieties fall into: fleur de sel, sel gris, flake salt, traditional salt, shio, rock salt, and smoked/infused salt.

Each of the salts that make up these broad categories look and taste like no other salt on earth, from mild to bold, from briny to sweet, from dry to moist, from delicate to rugged, from tactfully unprepossessing to ostentatiously gregarious. A single respectful glance at craft salt reveals something truly amazing: Salt has personality. Each has stories to tell that give our purchasing dollars meaning and make our cooking fulfilling.

The mission of this book is to make you think differently about salt and empower you to make food that is better in every way—taste, texture, eye appeal, and nutrition. My aims are to share an appreciation for real, naturally made salt and to reveal how the lively personalities of distinctive craft salts will celebrate your food like nothing else. With a pluck of courage, we can unearth the lost truth of craft salt, reveal its ancient power, and explore new horizons of flavor and satisfaction in cooking.

WINNING SALT

There are two ways to make salt. The most common salts are made by a process called winning, meaning evaporating salt water from the ocean, salt springs or wells, or from manmade brine. The other way is to dig it up out of the earth from a salt deposit.

Sea salts are the most common type of evaporative salt. Making them is simple enough, on paper: Collect some seawater in a shallow pond, keep it out of the rain, let the sun evaporate all the water, and then collect what's left. In reality it's fantastically more complicated than that. The process has to be controlled to crystallize the minerals you do want and leave behind the ones you don't. You need a lot of space dedicated to concentrating the seawater, and then a tidy, manageable area for crystallizing the salt and collecting it. If it rains, you're done for, so you need to pick the right place, and then scale everything to perfection so that you can make a reasonable quantity of salt before losing everything. If a storm comes, you lose the whole harvest, or worse, the entire salt farm.

Modernization has thrown up its own challenges, including the threat to salt marshes of urban development and pollution of the oceans. Perhaps the most difficult challenge faced by traditional sea salt farmers is the advent of large-scale, mechanized salt farming. Challenges notwithstanding, skilled practitioners of traditional solar salt making can be found around the globe. From Guatemala mangrove forests to highland Bolivia salt flats; from the Philippines to Vietnam; across Portugal, Spain, Italy, and Slovenia; from India to Eritrea to Ghana and a dozen countries in between, solar salt making is a vital economic activity and a storied connection to the past. Salt springs also feed famed salt works from Spain to Peru to China.

Lacking either an arid climate or natural concentrated brines, people have to get inventive. Bringing seawater into greenhouses both heats the brine and surrounding air to accelerate evaporation and protects the slowly forming salt from rain. This method has taken off in recent years in the Americas, where an often inhospitable climate and an insistence on sustainability converge to push salt makers to innovate. Hawaii, Maine, South Carolina, Florida, West Virginia, British Columbia, and Newfoundland are homes to greenhouse or similar zero-emissions salt-making techniques.

Yet another way to make salt sustainably is to look in the opposite direction of the sun, which is to say, straight down. Salt makers from Iceland to Wyoming to China have harnessed natural geothermal energy to make salt. The Earth's liquid mantle delivers more than twice the total of all humanity's energy output to Earth's

crust, superheating water that can be tapped at hot springs to heat pans filled with saltwater, creating exquisite salts in very inclement climates.

FIRE-EVAPORATED SALT

What do you do if you want to make salt, but there is simply not enough sun, too much rain, or no other natural sources of heat? The simple answer would be to boil off seawater using wood or coal or oil. This method was once widespread. Entire forests in Europe were decimated. Entire regions of England were blighted by coal soot. Thirty pounds of raw seawater must be evaporated to make a single pound of salt. The next time you reach for a box of fire-evaporated salt, consider that fossil fuels are a big part of the price tag!

Today environmental concerns make relying exclusively on fossil fuels to do the job unappealing and impractical in most instances, but there are exceptions. Many of the best fire-evaporated salts start with naturally concentrated brines, such as from a salt spring, well, or marsh, or use the limited available sun and wind to pre-evaporate the seawater to concentrate it before boiling off the remainder to crystallize salt. After 100,000 years of exploitation by Neolithic and post-Neolithic people in France, Le Briquetage de la Seille was developed and run as a major industrial salt works, boiling salt spring brine in earthenware vessels, breaking open the vessels to remove the cake of salt, and then discarding the vessels in heaps, converting at least 200 acres of the once flat countryside into a land of sprawling hills. People in China's Sichuan province have for millennia been pumping concentrated brine from 2,000-foot-deep wells in the earth. Neolithic England was home to salt making in its southern salt marshes—a practice that continues there today.

Where naturally concentrated brines are not available, ingenuity is required. The Japanese spray water onto bamboo mats suspended from the ceiling of a greenhouse, or drizzle water down long rods of bamboo, or even strew saltwater over seaweed or sand to allow it to quickly dry in the sun, then rinse the salt from the sand in seawater. A salt maker in Norway harnesses freezing weather rather than hot sun to concentrate saltwater. As seawater nears freezing, the water molecules crystallize, pushing the heavier saltwater to the bottom and yielding a concentrated brine that can then be evaporated by fire.

Some of the most desperate populations lack saltwater or salt deposits of any kind. In Paraguay, trees with a high salt content are burned, and the residual salt is rinsed from the ash and then boiled off. This same technique is practiced in Asia, Africa, and elsewhere, each locale burning its indigenous salty trees and grasses. One particularly innovative method, in the Philippines, involves soaking coconut husks in seawater for several months, drying and burning the coconut husks, washing the ash with saltwater to create a concentrated brine, and then boiling it off in a pot over a fire until nothing is left but a big round ball of salt. If you weren't convinced that mankind will do *anything* to get salt, these methods are proof.

The upshot is that spectacular salts can be made using either solar, fire, or hybrid methods. Solar (and geothermal) salts tend to be less expensive and more environmentally sustainable. For these reasons, solar salts are generally the best candidates for everyday cooking salts. Rock salts are also worth considering for use as an all-purpose salt, though for reasons we shall explore below, they may not be the ideal choice for many people.

ROCK SALT

The U.S. Geological Survey estimates the earth contains 332,519,000 cubic miles of water, 97 percent of which is saline. Every square mile contains 120 million tons of salt. Millions of years ago, much of the earth that today is land was buried under this saltwater. On occasion these ancient seas would become isolated as landmasses arose around them or as sea levels dropped during ice ages, stranding inland seas. These seas evaporated, leaving vast salt deposits that would eventually get buried under sediments and other geological formations. Under the tremendous pressure of the earth above, salt deposits would solidify into solid rock called halite, the mineral form of salt. The earth contains countless such salt deposits.

The Hallein salt mine in present-day Austria shows evidence of salt being evaporated from salt springs dating 4,000 years before organized rock salt mining of rock salt began there, around 600 BC. Two of the most famous salt mines in the world are the Wieliczka mine in Poland, near Krakow, and the Khewra mine in Pakistan's Punjab province. The Wieliczka mine (pronounced *vee-LEE-ska*) has been in operation since the 12th century. Intellectuals, dignitaries, and industrialists from around Europe have visited for centuries, and it is home to some of the most astonishing feats of minecraft anywhere. Caverns the size of small stadiums are buttressed by timbers stacked like Lincoln Logs. Animals were lowered down to the mine to work out their natural lives. Pulley systems, pump systems, stairways, elevators, tunnels, and halls weave throughout the byzantine maze of the mine. But here art rivals engineering for impressiveness. Miners, a religious and superstitious bunch, carved sculptures of everything from religious icons and personages to mythical dwarves, whom they believed contributed a helping hand, secretly working the mines at night. Mining of rock salt in Wieliczka recently ceased, but tourism continues.

The Khewra mine, in the Punjab region of Pakistan, is the largest of several in the region where so-called Himalayan salt comes from. The term *Himalayan* is a colorful one, as the mines are separated from the Himalayas by nearly 200 miles. The mines have been used since their discovery in 326 BC, and there is evidence to suggest that salt was being mined prior to that. Deep in its nearly 25 miles of tunnels winding through 43 square miles over seventeen levels, miners have carved elaborate structures and sculptures. Among them is a 350-foot-tall assembly hall with 300 narrow stairs of salt; a 3,000-square-foot mosque that was constructed over the course of half a century; and a salt bridge known as the Pull Sarat, or bridge of trial. It is 25 feet long, with no supporting pillars, spanning a subterranean saline pond. Other items include miniature versions of the Great Wall of China; the Eiffel Tower; and two Pakistani landmarks, Chaghi Mountain and Lahore's Minar-e-Pakistan. Khewra produces 300,000 tons per year. A good-size industrial salt mine might produce ten times that amount or more.

CRAFT VS. INDUSTRY: THE MODERN HISTORY OF SALT

The idea of good salt versus bad salt is not a new one. In the 1800s, the salt of choice was cheap, industrially made salt from Liverpool. Salt makers there boiled off brine using enormous amounts of cheap coal and other fossil fuels. Besides being an environmental catastrophe, the process yielded salt that many believed to be of middling quality at best. A letter circulated by the U.S. Senate in 1932 lambasted "the violent boiling and hasty crystallization" of "Liverpool salt, whose fair and tempting exterior renders it peculiarly imposing, whilst its intrinsic deficiency makes the delusional most pernicious and ruinous. . . . Indeed, this *artificial* salt is exceedingly unlike the salt formed by the evaporation and crystallization, which sea water *naturally* undergoes in the warmer latitudes." The letter continued on, lamenting its ruinous effect on beef, pork, and New York butter, among other foods. Such recognition is largely absent from discussions on salt today, but we are still besieged by inexpensive, inferior salt. Today it wallows in our food supply in the form of cheap sea salt, iodized table salt, and kosher salt.

KOSHER SALT AIN'T KOSHER

Kosher salt has been a longtime favorite in restaurants in the United States, and from there it became the darling of food magazines and many cookbook authors as well. What is strange is that kosher salt is an industrially compromised ingredient. Most serious cooks eschew heavily processed foods (bologna, corn syrup, Cheez Whiz) or artificial chemicals (red dye #5, vanillin, MSG) in their cooking. Kosher salt is both of those things. It is made by pumping water into a salt deposit, chemically refining the resulting brine, and then boiling it off in large factories using series vacuum evaporators fired by fossil fuels.

Another common rationale for using kosher salt is that it's cheap and readily available. This is true, but how much more expensive is it to use the best natural salt? A serving of superb natural salt costs about 3 cents, about the cost of a single slice of cucumber. Regardless of the cost, does "cheap and ubiquitous" express your aspirations as a cook? Excellent handcrafted salt is a luxury everyone deserves and can afford. Use salt that matters.

A WORD ON IODINE

Normally we get all the iodine we need from food, most notably seafood and dairy, but also beans, meat, and eggs. Sea vegetables, like seaweed salads, chips, or sheets, are so naturally high in iodine that they should actually be eaten in moderation. Salt is not, and never has been, a natural source of iodine.

Widespread access to seafood, dairy, and other iodine-rich foods has greatly reduced our need for iodine supplements. The British Dietetic Association states: "Most adults following a healthy, balanced diet that contains milk, dairy products, and fish should be able to meet their iodine requirements. A supplement containing iodine can help meet your iodine needs if you do not consume sufficient iodine-rich foods." Multivitamins and natural supplements at health food stores are convenient sources.

Where you should not be getting your iodine is from your salt. Relying on foods with additives for proper nutrition is deeply problematic. If we turn to cupcakes made with fortified flour for our vitamin B12, we are getting lots of things we don't need just to get a little of what we do need. The harsh, faintly acrid flavor of iodized salt should warn you off it.

A SEA SALT IS NOT A SEA SALT

Sea salt is a tricky one. What most people think when they say "sea salt" is something natural, pristine, and beautiful as the sea itself. What they are getting is another story altogether. Most generic sea salt is made on mega-farms like Exportadora de Sal in Baja California, which cranks out about 7 million tons a year, or Morton's Inagua salt fields in the Bahamas, which produce about 2 million tons a year. Cargill owns the largest sea salt operation in the United States, admired for its striking salt fields seen in the San

FOOD VS. CHEMICAL

Salt has been made to season food, preserve food, and supplement the diet of humans and livestock for thousands of years. About 270 million tons of salt are made every year—around 740,000 tons every day. However, salt for food and food processing makes up just 4 percent of the market, small potatoes next to the industrial uses for it.

In the mid-1800s salt found a new market, one that dwarfed its use in food. In the 1860s, Ernest Solvay perfected a method for making sodium carbonate (soda ash) by bubbling carbon dioxide through ammonia-containing salt brines. Today the world manufactures in the neighborhood of 50 million tons (45 million metric tons) of sodium carbonate, and its innumerable uses include dozens of chemical processes, water treatment, and making everything from detergents to paper to glass. The 1800s also saw the development of the chloralkali process for making chlorine and sodium hydroxide (caustic soda) from salt. Global chloralkali production is a staggering 200 million tons per year and growing. Gas exploration, pulp and paper making, metal processing, textile making and dyeing, tanning and leather treatment, rubber manufacture, and other industrial applications are the major uses. Road de-icing makes up yet another mega-market for salt, particularly in the United States.

Francisco Bay on approach to San Francisco International Airport. All of these makers share one goal: to make vast amounts of pure refined NaCl. These industrial sea salts are marketed as wholesome products made in harmony with nature, but in truth they rely on vast evaporating ponds that can undermine the sensitive ecological balance of their surroundings, and they require the use of heavy machinery, with all their attendant pollution. And the proof is in the pudding: At 99.8 percent pure NaCl, bereft of any of salt's natural minerals, this salt is more refined than any food it seasons.

THE CRAFT SALT FAMILY

We have been taught since childhood to think that salt is simple, but nothing could be further from the truth. Every craft salt has its own personality, and every personality is eager for an opportunity to harmonize (or clash) with your food. Rather than wade through an endless sea of different voices, we can combine them all into seven families: fleur de sel, sel gris, flake, traditional, shio, rock, and smoked and infused.

1. FLEUR DE SEL has delicate, moist, granular crystals and full mineral flavor. Fleur de sel forms when the weather is warm, and perhaps a light breeze tousles the surface waters of the crystallizing pan. Out of nowhere, salt crystals bloom across its face. In accommodating climates, fleur de sel crystals may sink and rest below the surface briefly, and then they are harvested before they have a chance to grow larger. The most important thing about fleur de sel is that the crystals are naturally fine, each as delicate and unique as a snowflake. Use it on milder, medium-bodied foods—everything from buttered toast to cooked vegetables to fish and pork.

2. SEL GRIS (also called *bay salt or gray salt*) boasts coarse, granular crystals with lots of moisture and rich, mineral flavor. Sel gris crystals form on the surface of a salt brine and also within the brine, and collect on the bottom. Sel gris is then raked off before it grows into a solid layer of salt, usually every several days. French sel gris is silvery gray from the trace amounts of silicates collected from the salt pan. Elsewhere, salt pans may be lined with a barrier against the mud below, or salt makers may allow a layer of salt to form on the bottom of the pan and then rake crystals off that layer. This produces very white salt that is nonetheless a sel gris. This is your salt for steak, lamb, root vegetables, and roasts of every kind.

3. FLAKE SALT comes in parchment-fine flecks and beautiful geometric pyramids. Flake salts are about fragility. The finest flake salts are so brittle that they pop into a million pieces if you so much as look at them the wrong way. Because they have very little mass for all that surface area, each crunch communicates only a smidge of salt. Some are moist; others are very dry. Though flake salts are most commonly made by evaporating water at a rapid rate, often at a boil, with fire or some other external heat source, there are a handful of flake salts made using only solar energy, usually in greenhouses. Flakes are incredibly variable from one maker to another, from one technique to another. Some form in tall, hollow pyramids, pointy as arrowheads, while others are squat pyramids, flat as Chinese throwing stars, and others are infinitesimally fine, like frost on the edge of a windowpane. Use them on fresh greens, cocktail rims, or anywhere a crisp, fleeting salt sensation is desired.

4. TRADITIONAL SALT (also referred to generically as *sea salt* and sometimes also *bay salt*) can be coarse or fine grained. Traditional salts are made similarly to fleur de sel and sel gris, except that rather than harvesting every day or several days, the salt is allowed to accumulate for months or even years. It is then harvested in huge chunks from a thick layer of salt accumulated on the bottom of a salt pan. The chunks are then mechanically ground down to the desired fineness. The salts can be made following any number of methods, from fire to geothermal to solar evaporation, though solar is by far the most common. Their use depends on the variety in question. Fine salts can be used as all-purpose cooking salts. Coarse salts can be used as a rustic touch on hearty foods.

5. SHIO is distinguished by fine to superfine grains. Named after the Japanese word for salt, shios are typically made in damp or cold climates where simple solar evaporation is not possible. Instead, salt water is pre-evaporated before being boiled or simmered into a concentrated brine over a fire; then the crystals are skimmed off the top or from within the brine. In short, it is made in much the same way as the best flake salts, except the crystals form in fine grains. Use shio on fish, steamed vegetables, in delicate broths, and—my favorite—in pickles.

6. ROCK SALT has hard, pebble-like crystals that can be ground to any coarseness. While many people consider rock salt to be the ultimate in natural, unrefined salts, in reality it is no more

or less pure than any good sea salt, and it is lower in minerals than many and has harder, less sensuous crystals than most. Rock salt is made by mechanically grinding rocks and boulders of salt found in the earth and running the results through screens to sift out the desired crystal size. **Rock salts, when finely ground, have excellent adhesion on fried foods like potato chips and french fries.**

7. SMOKED AND INFUSED SALTS can be made with virtually any salt, though flake salts and medium-ground to finely ground traditional salts are the most common. Smoked salts are made by cold-smoking wet salt crystals so they take up the rich, natural aroma of smoking woods. Mesquite, hickory, apple, alder, cherry—any aromatic wood can be used to smoke salt. Sprinkle them on food as a finishing touch to lend rich outdoorsy flavor. Infused salts are made in a variety of ways, but regardless of the technique, the best ones achieve something better than the sum of their parts. Like smoked salts, the best results are achieved by using them as a finishing touch. **Smoked and infused salts are for sprinkling wherever intense, high-fidelity flavor is desired.**

ANATOMY OF SALT

Four characteristics come into play when salt is used to cook and finish foods: crystal structure, moisture content, mineral content, and place of origin.

CRYSTAL STRUCTURE is the most important feature of any salt. Crystals can be chunky and coarse or granular and fine; they can be smooth and solid or intensely fractured; they can form into huge pyramidal structures that splinter into flakes or into superfine *fronds* and flecks that threaten to dissolve almost instantly. The importance of crystal structure cannot be overstated. Undissolved, it dictates the impact of the salt on your palate: the pop, crackle, snap that lend tantalizing crunch on a steak, crispy freshness on vegetables, or simmering subtlety on seafood.

MOISTURE CONTENT lends mouthfeel to salt crystals. Dried-out salt is hard. Moist salt is unctuous. A coarse, chunky salt with plenty of moisture yields to your tooth for a satisfying suppleness. Moist salts will loll about on the tongue, generating and mixing with your saliva, while dry salts will soak up every available drop of moisture in your mouth. The first sensation is nice. The second, often as not, is not. Moisture also lends resiliency to salt, so if you want a salt to resist dissolving on food long enough to make it into your mouth intact, moisture is key. Flake salts are the exception, as the big crystals of some flake salts perch on food without dissolving, then burst in your mouth without parching it.

MINERAL CONTENT varies enormously from salt to salt, from 3 percent to as much as 30 percent trace minerals. Where crystal structure and moisture contribute to the impact of the salt, minerals are what give salt its flavor. Every sea, every salt spring has its own unique mineral fingerprint. Distinct from the impact of the salt, this mineral profile imparts the salt's flavor. I call it "meroir"—akin to the terroir of wines. Some craft salts are briny, others are earthy; some are refined, others are harsh; some are sweet, others are bitter; and some are hot. Most are a combination of all of these sensations and more.

PLACE OF ORIGIN is a fourth consideration. While it does not directly affect your taste buds, it definitely affects the pleasure you take from your food. Place reflects our values. Place is a choice between farms or factories, sustainability or exploitation. And of course, places carry with them the thrill and romance of the flavors they evoke. A tagine redolent of Moroccan spices awakens an unconscious thrill of a North African moon rising over the Sahara. For me, fried garlic, steaming clams, and chopped parsley bring me back to a warm home for a linguine dinner with Mom. Salt is intimately connected to place, to natural environment, histories, and cuisines. The unique saltwater from which a salt is made, the unique climates that shape salts, and of course the unique people who do the salt making all resonate

THE INGREDIENT VS. THE COOK

Throughout history, cuisine has witnessed a power struggle between ingredient and technique. Love of ingredient shows us how to respect and honor the origin, people, and virtue of food. Expertise with technique shows us how to optimize, transform, and create as cooks. The silent integrity of the ingredient demands considered techniques to celebrate it. Think of the ingredient as the inspiration, and the technique as the creation. You can't have one without the other. When ingredients lack integrity, the creation lacks authenticity. Using cheap, poor-quality, industrialized ingredients will always make your food suffer. But using high-quality ingredients alone is not enough. To prepare truly delicious food, as opposed to the merely fashionable, surprising, or chic food, both technique and ingredient must shine, with neither outshining its partner.

"What do I want from my food?" That's the question you should ask every time you cook. Because salt enhances the flavor of almost any ingredient, anyone who eats on a regular basis eventually starts to salt by rote. Consider the interaction of your ingredients with the techniques you will use to prepare them. Think of salting as an opportunity. Do you want it to spark and vanish or persist and penetrate? Do you want to build a crescendo of flavor or do you prefer salt to barely underscore the flavors that are already present? What textures do you want: a quick snap, a subtle crackle, a just perceptible crunch, or nothing at all?

Consider that all food is not created equal. Even when cooking ingredients from the same food group, variations in cooking methods can yield vastly different dishes. The stewed flavors of a long-braised brisket are not the same as those of a grilled rare steak. Why salt them the same? Pasta sauced with foraged morels is nothing like the same noodle glistening with jewels of raw ripe tomato under a sheen of fruity olive oil. We need to recognize those differences and honor them with the considered application of distinctive salts. Salting purposefully deepens your connection to your ingredients, allowing you to cook them more considerately and creatively.

Making the most of every opportunity to use finishing salt is a matter of understanding the behaviors of different types of salts and then picking a salt that you think will fulfill the mission you set for it. For example, finish with a fleur de sel when you want delicacy and balance in every bite, or a flake salt when you want sparkle and contrast. Finish with sel gris when you want a powerful intonation that endures well after the fork has left your mouth, or finish with a smoked salt when you want the natural aromas of cooking outdoors to greet you before you've taken your first bite.

The importance of finishing with salt does not mean you shouldn't cook with it. A handful of traditional sea salt thrown into pasta water does wonders, and a sprinkling of fleur de sel an hour before grilling is the smartest thing you can do to up the ante on a thick steak. Stocks develop more flavor with salt. Vegetables brighten with salt in the water. Cookies may love salt sprinkled on top, but they need it in the dough, too.

THE THREE RULES OF SALTING

1. Cook with unsalted, whole foods whenever possible. Put yourself in the driver's seat so that you can do the salting, not some food chemist. Let *your* mouth decide when, where, and how much to salt. Salted butter is meh. Unsalted butter with fleur de sel is miraculous.

2. Use craft salt, and only craft salt, every day. It will cost you a few pennies more per person, but you'll be cooking like a king. Throw away your kosher salt, iodized table salt, and cheap sea salt. Salt brings pleasure. Your love is worth good salt.

3. Skew your salting toward the end of preparation, and use finishing salts. Use less or no salt while cooking, leaving room at the end to sprinkle a finishing salt of choice. Salt is the most powerful, distinctive ingredient. The right salt at the right time will celebrate your food like nothing else.

SALARIUS MAXIMUS

The purpose of salt is to elevate flavor and honor food. The best possible measure of a perfectly salted dish is not that it tastes salty, but that it tastes wonderfully, ecstatically like itself–or even better, like the dreamed-of ideal of itself. Salt makes pink fish taste like salmon, white roots taste like potato chips, and sweet dough taste like cookies. Sometimes, with outright aggressive salting, food can become something else altogether: an over-the-top, maddening sensation. A few recipes in this book tread the outer limits of sane salting, like the Fleur de Hell Fried Chicken (page 60), which employs a fine salt in the brine to moisten the meat and send the bird's savory flavors through the roof, a coarse salt in the breading for a glittering mineral zing, and a flake salt to finish just for the electrostatic crunch of it.

WHERE IS YOUR SALT?

If we took out all the salt put into food by factories and chefs, our salt consumption would shift radically; 75 percent of the salt we eat comes from processed or prepared foods. Only 10 percent of our dietary salt comes naturally in the foods we eat (and far less if you are a vegetarian), and typically only 15 percent from salt we add ourselves. The salient story here is eat processed and prepared foods less, cook whole foods yourself, then let fly with the salt, adding it judiciously but generously, freeing yourself to bring every bite to the peak of perfection.

Wowing as recipes like this can be, I'm not suggesting you make extreme salting a thematic part of your cooking. Adding too much salt can be like blasting the car radio to the point where the windows rattle as you drive down the street. The intensity of the experience drowns out the music. Remember, it's moderation we are seeking, though even moderation needs to be practiced in moderation.

My first book, *Salted: A Manifesto on the World's Most Essential Mineral, with Recipes,* is a celebration of salt, and the aim is to explore the untapped powers of the world's many distinctive varieties. Because nothing shows salt off like whole salt crystals atop a finished dish, techniques in the book were skewed toward finishing with salt rather than cooking with it. In this book I pick up where *Salted* leaves off, enlisting craft salt in a sweeping variety of salting techniques. As you work your way through the recipes here, I hope you will take note of the way we employ various techniques to push the boundaries of salting. Salt is frequently called upon several times in a recipe. You can blend a fine smoked salt with a chunky sel gris before rubbing it on a steak or chop like in the Thrice-Salted Rib-Eye Steaks (page 26). At other times, salting is a lesson in simplicity, like the Tossed Red Salad with Shallot Vinaigrette and Flake Salt (page 96). Show off some graphic panache with black and white salts atop Avocado Toast (page 95). For dessert, invite your mouth to a debate: White Chocolate Bark with Dark Chocolate Salt (page 137).

Like all chefs and many practiced home cooks, I add salt by pinches, not with measuring spoons, but in these recipes I have listed measurements of salt by teaspoon and tablespoon—not because I necessarily expect you to use them, but because it is the most accurate way of guiding you as you learn to salt purposefully.

Once you get the hang of it, I encourage you to go pro and stop wasting time digging for spoon measures. Your fingers will give you vital data about the salts you're using: their heft, their crunch, their moistness. As soon as you can, toss your measuring spoons out the window, but be cognizant of the risks. There is no way to rescue a dish once it has been oversalted. When you play with salt in your cooking, always be mindful of the total amount in any given recipe. Salting, like so much in life, is about judgment, but to live it to its fullest, it takes a little risk-taking.

CHARTING SALT

Before the recipes in each section you will find a quick reference table listing food compatibilities for each of the seven salt families, and a Salt Box follows almost every recipe, giving you alternatives to the salts found in the ingredient lists. A Craft Salt Field Guide (pages 152–161), organized by salt types, includes information about the individual types of salts found in this book.

SALT TABLE

Legend: Finishing: F Preparation: P Either: E

		Beef Steak	Beef Roast	Burgers	Pork Chop	Pork Roast	Lamb Chop	Lamb Roast	Braised Meat/Pot Roast	Roast Chicken/Turkey	Fried Chicken	Barbecue Chicken	Chicken Breast	Duck/Game Birds	Poached/Steamed Fish	Grilled Fish	Fried Fish	Eggs	Pancake/Waffle	Casserole/Enchilada	Cheese	Roasted (Baked) Vegetables	Fried Vegetables	Grilled Vegetables	Stir-Fry
Fleur de Sel		P	P	P	E	E	E	E		E	E	P	E		E	E	E	E	E	E	F	F	F	F	F
Sel Gris		E	E	F	F	E	F	E	E	P	P				E		E						F		
Flake Salt		F	F	F	F	F	F	F	F	F		F			F	F	F	F		F		F	F	F	F
Traditional Salt	Fine		P	P	P	P	P		P	P	P	P	E	P	P	P	P	P	P	E	P	P	P	E	P
	Coarse	F	F	P	F	F	F	F	F	P	E				F							F	F		
Shio				P							F		F	F	E	E	E	E				E	F	F	F
Rock Salt	Fine	P			P		P		P	P	P	P	E	P		P	P	P	E	P		P	P		
	Coarse		P					P	P																
	Salt Blocks, Bowls, Cups	E		P		P								P	P				P	P	F	P		P	
Infused	Smoked	P	P	P	P	P	P	P	P	P	P	P	E	P	E	P	E					F	F	F	
	Flavored	F	E	E	P	E	E	E	E	F	E	E	E	F	E	E	E	E	E	F	F	F	F	E	F
	Colored				F	F					F					F	F	F	F	F	F	F	F	F	F

FLEUR DE SEL
Delicately crunchy, fine grained for everyday cooking and sprinkling.

SEL GRIS
Coarse crystals with bold crunch and minerally flavor for hearty foods.

FLAKE SALT
Pyramidal confetti for snap and sparkle on fresh foods and cocktails.

TRADITIONAL SALT
Diverse family of salts made by hand in a time-honored fashion.

SALT TABLE

Legend: Finishing: F   Preparation: P   Either: E

		Pureed (Mashed) Vegetables	Green Salad	Raw Vegetable/Salad	Popcorn	Pasta	Rice/Other Grain	Firm Fruit (Apple, etc.)	Soft Fruit (Berries, etc.)	Melon	Soup/Stew	Bread	Pizza	Sandwich/Wrap	Fruit Dessert	Cookies	Cake	Ice Cream	Candy	Chocolate	Pudding/Custard	Pie	Sweet Drink	Refreshing Drink	Booze-Forward Drink
Fleur de Sel		E	E	F	F	E	E	F	F	F	P	P	P		F	E	E	E	E	E	E	E	E	F	F
Sel Gris		P				P					P			F				F							
Flake Salt			F	F				F	F	F	F			F	F	F	F	F	F	F	F	F	F	F	F
Traditional Salt	Fine	P		F	F	E	P	F	P		P	P	P				P	P	P	P	P	P		F	
	Coarse	E									P							P	F	F				F	
Shio			E	F	F	F	E	F	F	F	E				F			F	F	F			F	F	F
Rock Salt	Fine	P		F	F	E	E	F	P		P	P	P				P	P	P	P				F	
	Coarse					P	P				P	F	F			F		P	F						
	Salt Blocks, Bowls, Cups		F	F				F		F	P	P		E	P			P	P	P		P	F	F	
Infused	Smoked				F										F			F		F			F	F	F
	Flavored	F	F	F	F	F	F	F	F	F	F	F	F	F	F	F	F	F	F	F	F	F	F	F	
	Colored	F	F	F		F	F			F	F	F	F	F	F	F	F	F	F		F	F		F	

SHIO SALT
Fine, granular crystals harboring immense mineral richness.

ROCK SALT
Free-flowing crystals for baking, grinding, and shaking.

SMOKED SALT
Cold-smoked sea salt crystals for outdoorsy flavor and aroma.

INFUSED SALT
Select sea salt married with herbs and spices for an aromatic twist.

CHAPTER 1

MEAT

Salt on meat could be the most influential unrecorded recipe in recorded history–its simplicity makes it genius, and its complex play of texture, moisture, and primal flavor makes it eternal. Biting into a steak, juicy and salt crusted, you can imagine the bards of ancient times singing songs about battles and glory and love and home–and this is the food passed around the fire amidst. It was a single salt-studded steak eaten in a truck stop set along the rain-misted fields of northern France that first awoke me to the terrific power of craft salt. Like any great truth, salting meat is simple, but some basic rules apply.

There are three ways to salt meat:

1. Salting about 30 minutes before cooking will produce a thick pailletted crust.

2. Salting right after the meat comes off the heat will give you sparks of salinity punctuating unadorned flesh.

3. Applying salt in a cure over a period of days before cooking will fully alter the texture and flavor of meat, like with pastrami or sauerbraten.

The first two options above can be executed alone or in combination. The third option, curing, introduces enough salt that additional salting is rarely necessary. Meat can be cured either with a salt rub (sometimes called a dry brine) or by soaking meat in a saline bath, which is called a brine.

While there are only three primary ways to salt meat, the number of salts that can be used are nearly infinite. Using the right salt prior to cooking will have a big impact. Salting meat draws moisture to the surface. These meat juices are a mixture of water and savory liquefied proteins. Drawing a fine glaze of these juices to the surface of a roast, steak, or chop shortly before cooking is what creates a delectable crust. Sel gris, fleur de sel, or fine traditional salt are perfect for the job. The fine salt will draw just enough moisture to form an excellent crust. The coarser salts will only partially dissolve, thus drawing just enough moisture to form a crust, and the rest will wait patiently for the crunch of your bite. One salt that should not be used is kosher salt. Kosher salt, which is technically called koshering salt, does just that—it koshers, drawing out big puddles of moisture to create a soggy surface that resists crisping and crusting. The effect of kosher salt's unnaturally pure flecks of sodium chloride is closer to desiccation than encrustation.

The most controlled way to cook a steak is to sparingly preseason it to aid in crusting, and then to use a finishing salt at the table to deliver the perfect mineral contrast to each juicy bite. Enjoy the roar of larger crystal salts like sel gris, coarse traditional salt, and coarse flake salt, or tame things down with the purr of smaller crystals like fleur de sel and fine flake salt.

| | | | BEEF & LAMB | | | | | PORK & GAME | | | |
			roasted	grilled	fried	raw	cured	roasted	grilled	fried	cured
SALTS	fleur de sel		X	X	X	X	X	X		X	X
	sel gris		X	X			X	X			X
	flake	fine			X	X				X	
		coarse	X	X	X	X		X	X	X	
	traditional	fine			X	X	X	X	X		X
		coarse	X	X			X	X	X		X
	shio				X	X		X	X	X	X
	rock	fine					X			X	X
		coarse	X								
		block		X		X			X	X	
	infused	smoked	X	X	X		X	X	X	X	
		flavored	X	X	X			X	X	X	

Bistecca alla Fiorentina with Dolce di Cervia and Grilled Lemon

The famous steak from Florence is essentially a grilled porterhouse. To do it right, you will need a huge steak, around 2 inches thick. Most supermarkets don't usually cut steaks this thick, so you will probably have to call the meat department or your butcher ahead of time to order it. What makes it truly remarkable, however, is the simplicity of its seasoning—freshly ground pepper, a dousing of lemon juice, and a crunchy crust of the best salt you can find. For this recipe, I particularly love the "sale dolce," or "sweet salt" from the northern Adriatic. The big crunch and clean, almost fruity mineral flavor puts a stamp of authenticity on Bistecca alla Fiorentina that is as unmistakable as it is delicious.

Cut the lemon in half lengthwise. Squeeze the juice from half the lemon into a large resealable plastic bag. Reserve the other half. Add 3 tablespoons of the olive oil, 1 teaspoon of the sel gris, and ½ teaspoon of the pepper to the bag. Add the steak, press the air out of the bag, and seal the top. Massage the marinade into the meat and refrigerate for at least 6 hours or up to 24 hours.

When ready to grill, remove the marinating steak from the refrigerator and set out at room temperature for 1 hour. Soak the wood chips in cold water for at least 30 minutes.

Meanwhile, set up your grill—if using charcoal, make a hot fire (about 500°F) covering one half of the grill bed. If using a gas grill, turn half of the burners on high and leave the other half off.

When ready to cook, remove the steak from the marinade and discard the marinade. Drain the wood chips and scatter over the hot coals. If using a gas grill without a smoker box, put the chips in aluminum foil and poke holes in the foil, then put the foil directly over one of the gas burners. If you have a smoker box on your grill, use it.

- 1 large lemon
- ¼ cup extra-virgin olive oil, divided
- 1 tablespoon sel gris or coarse traditional salt such as Dolce di Cervia, divided
- 1 teaspoon coarsely ground black pepper, divided
- 1 (2½ to 3-pound) large porterhouse or T-bone steak, at least 2 inches thick
- 1 cup oak or hickory wood chips or chunks
- Mild vegetable oil, for coating grill grate

Continued

Brush the grill grate with vegetable oil, then grill the steak directly over the fire with the lid down until darkly crusted, 4 to 6 minutes per side. Sprinkle all over with the remaining 2 teaspoons of sel gris and ½ teaspoon of pepper as you turn the steak.

Move the steak to the part of the grill without a fire, cover the grill, and cook for another 6 to 12 minutes for medium-rare to medium. Transfer to a platter, loosely cover with foil, and let rest for 5 to 8 minutes.

While the steak rests, coat the reserved lemon half with a bit of olive oil and grill, cut side down, over direct heat until nicely grill-marked, 1 to 2 minutes. Cool slightly, then cut the lemon into 4 thin wedges.

Make individual servings by cutting both sections away from the bone, then cutting them into 4 to 6 pieces, or by cutting all of the meat into ½-inch-thick slices and serving each guest a mix of tenderloin and top loin slices. (The bone itself is up for grabs.) Serve with the remaining olive oil drizzled over the top and the grilled lemon wedges.

SALT BOX

Piran Sel Gris; Sel Gris de Noirmoutier, Guérande, or l'Île de Ré; Kona Deep Sea Salt; Fiore di Trapani, Sal de Ibiza Granito

Thrice-Salted Rib-Eye Steaks with Brown Butter Aioli

MAKES 4 SERVINGS

Even though all salts are salty, they vary dramatically in key directions, making it not only possible but also easy to build diversity in a single dish with salt alone. This rustic steak is a case in point: seasoned with smoke; textured with crunchy chunks of solidified brine, some sweetly minerally, others boldly smoky; and finished with massive saline shards of munchable black wrought iron.

STEAKS

1 tablespoon smoked salt

1 tablespoon sel gris or coarse traditional salt

1 teaspoon freshly ground black pepper

½ teaspoon ground mustard

½ teaspoon garlic powder

½ teaspoon onion powder

4 (8 to 10-ounce) boneless beef rib-eye steaks, about 1 inch thick

2 tablespoons unsalted butter

AIOLI

6 tablespoons unsalted butter

3 medium cloves garlic, coarsely chopped

½ teaspoon medium-grained sea salt (such as a fleur de sel of choice)

2 large egg yolks

2 tablespoons fresh lemon juice

2 tablespoons boiling water

4 pinches black salt

To prepare the steaks, mix the salts, pepper, mustard, and garlic and onion powders together in a bowl. Season both sides of all of the steaks; set aside for at least 15 minutes.

Heat the butter in a cast-iron skillet over medium-high heat. Cook the steaks in the hot butter until browned on both sides and the steaks barely feel resilient in the center, medium-rare, about 5 minutes per side. Transfer the steaks to a serving platter; cover loosely with aluminum foil to keep warm.

To make the aioli, wipe out the skillet. Add the butter to the pan and cook over medium heat until the butter turns golden brown, about 3 minutes. Remove from the heat.

Mash the garlic and sea salt on a cutting board into a smooth paste. Transfer to a medium bowl. Add the egg yolks and lemon juice, and mix well with a whisk. Slowly drizzle the melted butter into the yolks, mixing it in drop by drop. The mixture will thicken into a creamy, pourable sauce. When it gets too thick to pour, add the boiling water.

Serve each steak with some sauce and a scattering of black salt.

SALT BOX

Smoked Salt: Vancouver Island Smoked Sea Salt, Bulls Bay Bourbon Barrel Smoked Flake, Halen Môn Gold Sea Salt, Maine Apple Smoked Sea Salt
Sel Gris: Sel Gris de Guérande, l'Île de Ré, or Noirmoutier
Traditional Coarse Salt: Amagansett Sea Salt, Dolce di Cervia
Black Salt: Icelandic Lava Salt, Kilauea Onyx Sea Salt, Black Lava Salt, Black Diamond Flake Salt

Umami Burgers with Moshio

MAKES 4 SERVINGS

Your mouth can pick up five tastes—sweet, salty, sour, bitter, and umami. Umami tastes savory like roasted meat or sautéed mushrooms. In Japanese, *umami* translates roughly as "deliciousness," and it has been recognized in Japan as a unique taste since 1908. It was not until 2001 that western science confirmed the existence of specialized taste receptors on the tongue for umami. Moshio is a crazy-delicious salt made by evaporating salt with seaweed, and the wonder twins activate to form an umami-salty tsunami that will take your burgers over the top.

2 tablespoons finely chopped dried porcini mushrooms (3 or 4 medium pieces; 4 g/0.14 ounce)

2 tablespoons soy sauce

3 tablespoons hot water

1 teaspoon anchovy paste

2 teaspoons tomato paste

½ teaspoon black pepper

1½ pounds ground beef chuck, 85% lean

Olive oil, for coating grill grate

1½ teaspoons Moshio salt

4 hamburger buns, split

2 tablespoons chopped pickled ginger

12 thin slices cucumber

Mix the mushrooms, soy sauce, and hot water in a medium bowl. Set aside for a minute to soften the mushrooms. Stir in the anchovy paste, tomato paste, and pepper. Add the beef and mix with your hands just until blended. Using a light touch, form into 4 patties about ¾ inch thick and 4 inches in diameter. Pinch a quarter-size dimple in the center of each patty. As the burgers grill, they will shrink in from the edges, causing the center to swell. By making a divot in the center of the raw patty, you end up with a grilled burger that is flat and even, perfect for stacking on the garnishes. Refrigerate until ready to grill.

Preheat a charcoal or gas grill for medium direct heat (350° to 400°F). Clean the grill grate with a metal brush and coat the grate with olive oil.

Season the burgers all over with 1 teaspoon of the salt and put on the grill. Cover and cook for 9 minutes, flipping after 5 minutes for medium (150°F for slightly pink). Add a minute per side for well-done (160°F).

To toast the buns, put them cut sides down directly over the fire for the last minute of cooking.

If serving the burgers directly from the grill, serve on buns topped with the pickled ginger and sliced cucumbers and sprinkled with the remaining ½ teaspoon of salt. If the burgers will sit, even for a few minutes, keep buns and burgers separate until just before eating.

> ## SALT BOX
> Tsushima No Moshio, Amabito No Moshio, Kamebishi Soy Salt, Sal de Gusano

Roasted Prime Rib with Garlic and Pink Rock Salt

MAKES 8 TO 10 SERVINGS

Prime rib is nobody's everyday meal. It's a celebration. Whether you are at a restaurant or at home, its arrival at the table makes you feel like a king. The only difference is that you can have it better at home. High-quality salt is like setting out the fine silver; it honors the food and elevates the occasion. Compared to evaporated sea salts, rock salts are hard and flinty—just the consistency you want to stand up to long hours in the oven, so that every lovingly carved slice still bristles with bright beads of salinity.

Slip the garlic slivers between the meat and fat on the top of the roast, and between the meat and bones on the bottom. Season the roast all over with 2 teaspoons of the salt and the two peppers; set in the refrigerator, uncovered, for 12 to 24 hours. Remove from the refrigerator 1 hour before you plan to start roasting.

Preheat the oven to 550°F.

Place the beef in a large metal roasting pan, fat side up, and sprinkle with the remaining 1 teaspoon salt, pressing the salt into the fat layer to help it adhere. Put the meat in the oven and roast for about 20 minutes, or until the surface starts to brown. Decrease the oven temperature to 170°F and roast until an instant-read thermometer inserted into the center of the meat registers 135°F, about 4 hours. Because the shape of the roast affects the rate of heat transference through the meat, start checking for doneness at 3 hours to make sure you don't overcook the roast.

Transfer the meat to a carving board, and let rest for 15 to 25 minutes before slicing and serving.

6 cloves garlic, slivered

1 (4-rib) standing beef rib roast, about 8 pounds

1 tablespoon coarse Himalayan Pink Salt, divided

1 teaspoon coarsely ground black pepper

1 teaspoon cracked dried green peppercorns

SALT BOX

Persian Blue Salt, Brazilian Sal Grosso, Redmond Real Salt, Oryx Desert Smoked Salt

Colorado Beef Burgers
with Mesquite-Smoked Salt and Chiles

MAKES 6 SERVINGS

Mesquite wood derives its strength through deprivation. Gnarly and implacable mesquite thrives in the desert with little water and even less cultivation. Its wood burns superhot, billowing an abundance of pungent smoke that invades anything that gets in its way, tenaciously clinging even to rock-hard salt crystals. This profoundly flavorful and simple burger draws its smoke from three sources: chipotle chiles (smoked jalapeños), a raging charcoal fire, and mesquite-smoked salt. Ours is made in small batches on the Maine coast.

2 pounds ground beef chuck, 85% lean

5 tablespoons ice-cold water

1 tablespoon chipotle hot sauce, divided

1½ teaspoons mesquite-smoked salt

½ teaspoon freshly ground black pepper

¼ cup mayonnaise

Mild vegetable oil, for coating grill grate

12 slices good-quality pepper Jack cheese (optional)

6 hamburger buns, split

6 Hatch chiles, stemmed, seeded, and thinly sliced

Heat a grill for medium-high direct heat (400° to 450°F).

Mix the beef, water, 1 teaspoon of the chipotle hot sauce, salt, and pepper in a bowl until well blended; do not overmix. Gently form the meat into 6 patties no more than 1 inch thick. Pinch a quarter-size dimple in the center of each patty. By making a divot in the center, you end up with a grilled burger that is flat and even, perfect for stacking on the garnishes. Refrigerate the burgers until the grill is ready.

In the meantime, mix the mayonnaise with the remaining 2 teaspoons of chipotle hot sauce. Set aside until ready to use.

Brush the grill grate and coat with oil. Put the burgers on the grill, cover, and cook for 7 minutes, turning after about 4 minutes for medium (150°F for slightly pink). Add a minute per side for well-done (160°F).

If you are making cheeseburgers, put 2 slices of cheese on each burger 1 minute before the burgers are going to be done.

To toast the buns, put them cut sides down directly over the fire 1 minute before the burgers are going to be done. If serving the burgers directly from the grill, serve on buns with sliced chiles and chipotle mayo. If the burgers will sit, even for a few minutes, keep the buns and burgers separate until just before eating.

Sel Gris Pastrami

MAKES ABOUT 8 SERVINGS

In 1962 there were more than 2,000 Jewish-style delicatessens in New York City. Now there are less than a thousand in the whole country. True deli is a vanishing art that follows a time-consuming, labor-intensive process of smoking, curing, pickling, and spicing that predates refrigeration. Nowadays if you want top-notch pastrami, you might have to make it yourself. Fortunately, though DIY pastrami takes time, it doesn't take a lot of effort, and if you switch from kosher salt to sel gris, the results far surpass what you can get at the corner deli.

4 pounds uncooked corned beef

2 tablespoons large sel gris (such as Sel Gris de Noirmoutier)

2 tablespoons black peppercorns, cracked

2 tablespoons coriander seeds, cracked

180 cubic inches (3 quarts) hardwood chips (such as alder, cherry, or apple)

1 small loaf fresh rye bread

½ cup grated horseradish

⅓ cup spicy brown mustard

SALT BOX

Any coarse traditional salt or sel gris will do here. Favorites include Piran Sel Gris, Dolce di Cervia, Yellowstone Natural Salt, and any French sel gris.

Remove the corned beef from its brine; wash in 3 to 6 changes of cold water to desalinate the meat a bit. Pat dry.

Mix the sel gris, peppercorns, and coriander seeds. Coat the meat with the mixture, pressing the rub into the surface of the meat. Put on a rack and refrigerate for 1 to 24 hours.

Set up a smoker (either charcoal or electric) to about 225°F. Add the wood chips according to the smoker's directions. Place the pastrami fat side up on a rack set above a pan of water and smoke until an instant-read thermometer inserted into its thickest part registers 190° to 200°F, about 6 hours. You will have to replenish the wood chips every 2 hours, and, if using charcoal, the charcoal at the same time.

Remove the pastrami from the smoker. Wrap the pastrami in plastic wrap and refrigerate it overnight. (At this point, it will keep for up to 1 week.)

To steam, put the pastrami in a metal or bamboo steamer and steam over barely simmering water until an instant-read thermometer inserted into its thickest part registers about 205°F, about 40 minutes. Slice it into ⅛-inch-thick slices perpendicular to the grain of the meat.

Serve with the bread, horseradish, and mustard.

Venison Steak with Takesumi Bamboo Sea Salt

MAKES 4 SERVINGS

My first meal with Takesumi Bamboo Salt was bourbon-glazed venison on a plate dotted casually around its rim with molten-hot jalapeño pepper and little volcanoes of Takesumi Bamboo piled by its side. Never in my experience have color, flavor, and texture been so implausibly and perfectly married. I have no idea how the chef who created the inspiration for this recipe wove his magic, but I think we got pretty damn close.

Turn a gas burner or a broiler to high. Perch the jalapeños on the burner grate directly over the fire, or on a broiler pan placed directly under the fire, and cook until the skin on the peppers chars, turning to get an even blackening on all sides, about 2 minutes per side. Cool. Cut off the stem ends; remove the seeds if you want to soften their heat.

Put the bourbon, jalapeños, honey, thyme, and garlic in a food processor and process into a fine purée. Add the pepper flakes and olive oil. Wrap in plastic wrap and refrigerate for about 6 hours.

Heat a grill for direct medium-high heat, about 450°F.

Brush the grill grate and coat with vegetable oil. Pat the venison steaks to remove any obvious moisture, but keep as much of the bourbon paste on the meat as you can; sprinkle with 1 teaspoon of the salt and the pepper. Grill directly over the heat for 2 to 4 minutes per side for rare to medium-rare (130° to 135°F internal temperature). Remove and let rest for 3 minutes. Sprinkle with the remaining 1 teaspoon of salt and serve.

3 jalapeño chiles

¼ cup bourbon

1 tablespoon honey

8 sprigs thyme

4 cloves garlic, peeled

¼ teaspoon red pepper flakes (optional)

¼ cup extra-virgin olive oil

8 deer tenderloin steaks, about ¾ inch thick

Mild vegetable oil, for coating grill grate

2 teaspoons Takesumi Bamboo Sea Salt

½ teaspoon coarsely ground black pepper

SALT BOX

Takesumi Bamboo Sea Salt is unlike any other salt. If none is at hand, try Black Lava Salt, or use Flos Salis, Piran Fleur de Sel, or Fleur de Sel de l'Île de Ré.

Heritage Pork Chops with Red Salt and Black Salt Roasted Corn Relish

MAKES 4 SERVINGS

Man has been breeding pigs since as far back as 11,000 years ago, but there was no such thing as heritage pork until the modern pork industry started messing with nature, creating leaner and leaner pigs that turned into blander and blander meat. The choice to reclaim old established breeds, like Berkshire and Hampshire, which produce well-marbled, juicy, dark-fleshed pork chops, is just a matter of good taste. If you don't know the breed of pig your pork is coming from, look for "pastured" or "free-range" pork. Haleakala Ruby and Kilauea Onyx, not to be confused with the cheap knockoff red salts made to look like real McCoy, are big and rich and buttery, and made entirely by hand: heritage salt.

2 tablespoons blackstrap molasses

1 tablespoon apple cider vinegar

4 bone-in heritage pork rib chops, 1 to 1½ inches thick, about 3 pounds total, trimmed of excess fat

2 teaspoons red salt, divided

2 teaspoons black salt, divided

2 tablespoons extra-virgin olive oil, divided

3 ears fresh corn, husks removed

1 small tomato, seeded and finely chopped

1 jalapeño chile, seeded and finely chopped

1 small clove garlic, minced

2 tablespoons chopped red onion

2 tablespoons chopped fresh cilantro

Juice of ½ lime

½ teaspoon freshly ground black pepper

Mix the molasses and vinegar together in a small bowl. Brush the chops with this mixture. Sprinkle with 1 teaspoon of each of the salts and set on a rack set on a sheet pan in the refrigerator for at least 1 hour or up to 1 day.

Preheat the oven to 450°F.

Coat the corn with 1 tablespoon of the olive oil. Roast until browned, about 15 minutes. Set aside to cool.

Combine the tomato, jalapeño, garlic, onion, cilantro, lime juice, and pepper in a medium bowl. Cut the corn kernels from their cobs and toss with the vegetables and the remaining 1 teaspoon of each of the salts.

Decrease the oven temperature to 350°F. Heat the remaining 1 tablespoon of olive oil in a large cast-iron skillet over high heat. Put the chops in the hot pan and brown on both sides, about 2 minutes per side. Move to the oven and roast until an instant-read thermometer inserted into the thickest chop register 154°F, about 15 minutes. Serve the chops topped with the relish.

SALT BOX

Red Salt: **Haleakala Ruby Sea Salt, Molokai Red Sea Salt, or go pale with silvery Piran Sel Gris or rosy Sugpo Asin.**
Black Salt: **Kilauea Onyx Sea Salt, Icelandic Lava Salt, Black Lava Salt**

Barbecue Spare Ribs with Sweet Smoked Brine

MAKES 6 SERVINGS

The golden general rule of salting is to give salt a voice, and to do that it's best to salt toward the end of your food preparation. The sumptuous charm of a roasted rib of beef or charred steak depends on the dynamic contrast between a crackling salt-studded crust and its virginally rare interior. But barbecue doesn't give a damn about golden rules. The allure of barbecue is the permutation of smoke and spice throughout. Barbecue is one place where salt enters in the beginning, the middle, and the end. You do not finish barbecue with great salt—you inundate it every step of the way.

ALDER RUB

3 tablespoons smoked paprika

3 tablespoons dark brown sugar

3 tablespoons alder smoked salt

1½ tablespoons freshly ground black pepper

1½ tablespoons chipotle chile powder

BRINE

2 cups apple cider or juice

⅔ cup hard cider or lager beer

⅓ cup apple cider vinegar

¼ cup Alder Rub

2 tablespoons smoked salt of choice

2 slabs pork ribs, baby back or St. Louis cut, about 4 pounds total

BBQ SAUCE

¼ cup apple cider or juice

¼ cup apple cider vinegar

¼ cup ketchup

2 tablespoons spicy brown mustard

2 tablespoons honey

1 to 2 tablespoons habanero hot sauce

½ teaspoon freshly ground black pepper

½ teaspoon smoked salt of choice

Continued

For the rub, mix all of the ingredients in a small bowl; set aside. The rub can be stored in a refrigerator for up to 1 week.

For the ribs, combine the brine ingredients in a gallon-size resealable plastic bag, mixing with a whisk to dissolve the salt. Cut the racks in half, between the 6th and 7th ribs. Put in the bag with the brine. Seal the zipper, leaving about an inch open; push on the bag to release any trapped air through the opening, and close the zipper completely. Massage the liquid gently into the meat and refrigerate for 6 to 12 hours.

For the sauce, mix all of the ingredients together in a medium saucepan. Bring to a boil and simmer until lightly thickened, about 5 minutes; store in the refrigerator in a tightly closed container for up to 1 month.

Remove the ribs from the brine and pat dry. Season the ribs all over with the remaining ½ cup of rub. Set aside for at least 15 minutes, or refrigerate for up to 12 hours.

Preheat a charcoal or gas grill for medium indirect heat (300° to 350°F).

Clean the grill grate with a wire brush and put the ribs, bone side down, on the grill away from the heat. Cover the grill and cook until an instant-read thermometer inserted into the thickest part of the ribs registers about 180°F, 50 minutes to 1 hour.

When the ribs are done, brush the tops with a generous glaze of the sauce, using about half of the sauce (about ⅔ cup). Cover the grill and cook for about 4 minutes, or until the glaze is set.

Transfer the ribs to a large serving board and cut into 1 or 2-rib pieces. Serve with the remaining sauce for dipping.

Pulled Lamb Flatbreads with Pomegranate Syrup and Lemon Salt

MAKES 6 SERVINGS

Now that McDonald's has joined Wendy's and Burger King in embracing the pulled pork sandwich, it seems like the perfect moment for all us thinking people to satisfy our pulled meat jones elsewhere. I vote for lamb shoulder. It's as flavorful and as rich as pork and way more interesting. In this recipe, we braise lamb shoulder with lemon salt and spices until it literally falls into shreds. Then we tuck it into a pita pocket, top it with caramelized onions inundated with pomegranate syrup made from the reduced braising juices, and scatter on a few more shards of lemon salt flakes.

1 tablespoon ground cumin

1 tablespoon ground coriander

1 tablespoon curry powder

1 tablespoon crushed dried rosemary

1 teaspoon red pepper flakes

4 teaspoons lemon salt, divided

1 teaspoon freshly ground black pepper

1 (4 to 5-pound) boneless lamb shoulder

2 tablespoons olive oil

3 medium yellow onions, halved and thinly sliced

3 cloves garlic, sliced

2 cups pomegranate juice

3 tablespoons honey, divided

6 pita breads

1 cup plain Greek yogurt

¼ cup orange juice

½ cup pomegranate seeds

¼ cup chopped fresh mint leaves

Continued

Mix the cumin, coriander, curry powder, rosemary, pepper flakes, 1 tablespoon of the lemon salt, and black pepper together in a small bowl. Rub half all over the lamb. Wrap in plastic wrap and refrigerate for 24 hours.

Preheat the oven to 200°F.

Heat the olive oil in a Dutch oven large enough to hold the lamb snugly over medium-high heat. Add the lamb and brown on all sides, about 4 minutes per side. Transfer to a platter.

Add the onions to the pan and sauté until browned, about 10 minutes, stirring often. Add the remaining half of the spice mixture and the garlic, and sauté for another minute. Return the lamb to the pot, along with any juices that have collected on the platter. Pour the pomegranate juice over all. Cover the pan and bake until the lamb is fork-tender, about 5 hours.

Pour the meaty pomegranate juices into a deep skillet. Turn the oven up to 400°F and return the pot of lamb to the oven, uncovered, until the top is crisped, about 15 minutes.

Skim the fat from the meaty pomegranate juices in the skillet and stir in 2 tablespoons of the honey. Boil over medium-high heat until the liquid is reduced to 2 cups (about half), about 10 minutes.

Transfer the lamb to a cutting board. Slice the lamb against its grain into 1-inch-thick slices. With 2 forks, pull apart into shreds. Mix 1¼ cups of the reduced pomegranate juices into the lamb and keep warm.

SALT BOX

Any number of aromatic salts will marry beautifully with this spiced lamb dish: Rosemary Flake Salt, Blue Lavender Flake Salt, or Pinot Noir Sea Salt. Noninfused crispy flake salts will work nicely, too: Icelandic Flake Salt, Havsnø Flaksalt, Hana Flake Salt, Alaska Pure Sea Salt, or Halen Môn Silver Flake Sea Salt.

Warm the pitas in the oven. Add the remaining pomegranate juices to the onions in the Dutch oven and simmer over medium heat until the mixture is slightly thickened, about 5 minutes.

Mix the yogurt, orange juice, remaining 1 tablespoon of honey, pomegranate seeds, and mint leaves together.

Serve piles of pulled lamb on warm pita topped with syrupy onions, the pomegranate-mint yogurt, and a sprinkle of the remaining 1 teaspoon of lemon salt.

Roast Leg of Lamb with Tomatoes, Fennel, and Saffron Salt

MAKES 10 TO 12 SERVINGS

No one knows lamb like the Greeks, Turks, and Arabs of the Middle East. The flavors in this recipe are reminiscent of how Bedouin nomads might spit-roast a leg of lamb over a live fire. Let's bring the whole process indoors, marinating the leg in yogurt and spices overnight and then roasting it the next day (or the day after the next day, depending on your schedule), gilding the finished roast with saffron salt. It is our opinion that lamb should never be cooked past medium-rare (135°F). Past that point, it loses its succulence and begins to take on the livery flavors that folks who say they hate lamb think it tastes like.

MARINADE

2 cups buttermilk or plain yogurt

1 cup orange juice

¼ cup extra-virgin olive oil

8 cloves garlic, sliced

2 tablespoons chopped fresh rosemary leaves

2 tablespoons crushed cardamom seeds

1 tablespoon saffron salt

1 teaspoon freshly ground black pepper

¼ teaspoon red pepper flakes

LAMB

1 whole bone-in leg of lamb, 7 to 8 pounds (see Note)

2 tablespoons extra-virgin olive oil

4 carrots, peeled and diced

4 ribs fennel, diced

2 medium yellow onions, diced

4 cloves garlic, minced

2 tablespoons fresh thyme leaves

2 teaspoons crushed cardamom seeds

1 (14.5-ounce) can diced tomatoes, undrained

¾ cup orange juice

1 tablespoon saffron salt

2 teaspoons coarsely ground black pepper, divided

¼ cup chopped fresh flat-leaf parsley

1 tablespoon finely grated orange zest

Mix all of the ingredients for the marinade in a large bowl. Put the lamb in a jumbo resealable plastic bag, at least 2 gallons, or you can double up 2 large kitchen trash bags. Add the marinade; massage the marinade into the meat briefly. Close the bag, squeezing out as much of the air as you can without letting any marinade seep from the opening, and seal the bag. Refrigerate for 24 to 48 hours.

Preheat the oven to 450°F.

While the oven is preheating, heat the olive oil in a large skillet over medium-high heat. Add the carrots, fennel, and onion, and sauté until the vegetables brown lightly, about 10 minutes. Stir in the garlic and sauté for another 30 seconds. Stir in the thyme, cardamom, tomatoes, orange juice, 1 teaspoon of the saffron salt, and 1 teaspoon of the pepper. Bring to a boil and remove from the heat.

Remove the lamb from the marinade. Pat off any excess marinade from the surface; moisture on the surface of the meat will inhibit its ability to brown. Put on a rack set in a roasting pan large enough to hold the lamb. Roast for 30 minutes.

Turn the oven down to 300°F. Pour the tomato mixture over the meat and roast until an instant-read thermometer inserted into the thickest part of the meat registers about 135°F for medium-rare, about 1 hour and 15 minutes.

Transfer the lamb to a large carving board; set aside to rest for 10 minutes. Skim the fat from the pan juices and stir in the parsley and orange zest.

Carve the lamb and sprinkle the slices with just enough of the remaining 2 teaspoons of saffron salt and 1 teaspoon of pepper to show off the dish. Spoon the braised vegetables around the roasted meat and serve the roasting juices on the side.

Note: Unlike the legs of larger animals, a primal leg of lamb is sold with the hip bone still attached, which gives the roast a dramatic shape but can be more problematic for carving.

> ## SALT BOX
>
> There is no substitute for saffron. Attempts to describe its aroma never fail to include the hay, but it's saffron's profound weirdness that drives us, a carnal reverie of sweat, hammock strings, and driftwood washed ashore to dry in the sun. There is no substitute for saffron, except for Saffron Salt.

CHAPTER 2

POULTRY

Salting a bird's tail may be a fruitless way to catch it (although if you are close enough to start salting the tail feathers, you're probably in a good position to grab the whole bird), but sprinkling salt anywhere else on poultry is definitely a good idea.

There are three ways to salt poultry:

1. Sprinkling coarse salt all over the raw bird or its parts and refrigerating it, uncovered, for several hours (or better yet, overnight) will dry the surface of bone-in poultry and help the skin crisp and brown during roasting.

2. Soaking the raw meat in a brine solution of 1¼ tablespoons fine salt dissolved in every cup of water will increase the juiciness of cooked poultry, particularly breast meat.

3. Adding a rough-textured salt, like flake salt or sel gris, immediately after your bird comes off the heat will create sparks of salinity in every bite.

It goes without saying that proper salting will enhance the intrinsic avian flavor of the bird. More and more mainstream poultry producers are offering free-range chickens, which do get a chance to peck outside at corn thrown from an actual farmer's hand. They generally get more exercise and have the opportunity for exposure to the sun. Their meat genuinely tastes more like chicken than traditionally cooped birds, but you'll likely pay nearly twice as much as you'll pay for their mass-produced competition.

SALTS			CHICKEN			GAME			DUCK		
			roasted	grilled	fried	roasted	grilled	fried	roasted	grilled	fried
	fleur de sel		x	x	x	x	x	x	x	x	
	sel gris			x						x	x
	flake	fine	x	x	x	x	x	x	x	x	x
		coarse	x	x			x				
	traditional	fine	x	x	x	x	x	x	x		x
		coarse		x							
	shio				x			x	x		x
	rock	fine			x			x			x
		coarse	x								
		block		x		x	x			x	
	infused	smoked	x			x	x	x	x		
		flavored	x	x		x	x		x	x	

Korean Bamboo Barbecue Chicken with Toasted Sesame Salt

MAKES 4 SERVINGS

Barbecue is slow roasting with an open fire. Here, this technique is mixed with Korean flavors assembled from tangy pineapple juice, a hefty dollop of gochujang (Korean chili paste), and a salt that has fire in its very DNA. Bamboo salt is a traditional Korean salt made by packing sea salt into canisters of giant bamboo, capping it with yellow clay, baking it in an iron oven, and finally roasting it in a pine fire. The results speak for themselves: rich, full, slightly umami, rounded with an eggy sulfuric element. The Koreans believe these five elements—salt, plant, earth, iron, and fire—combine in this single ingredient to produce chi that is beneficial for the mind and soul.

Mix 2 cups of the pineapple juice, 5 teaspoons of the bamboo salt, and 2 tablespoons of the gochujang in a jumbo (2-gallon) resealable plastic bag until the salt dissolves. Add the chicken pieces. Seal the zipper, leaving about an inch open; push on the bag to release any trapped air through the opening, and close the zipper completely. Massage the liquid gently into the chicken and refrigerate for 6 to 12 hours.

Light a grill for indirect medium heat, about 325°F. If you are using a charcoal grill, this means banking your coal bed to one side or at opposite ends of the fire box, leaving an area open that's large enough to hold the racks of ribs. If you have a two-burner gas grill, turn one side on to medium and leave the other side off. If you have a three-burner or more grill, turn the outside burners on to medium and leave the center burner(s) off.

Brush the grill grate and coat with oil. Put a pan of water directly over the fire. Remove the chicken from the brine and discard the brine. Put the chicken on the grill, skin side up, away from the heat, with the dark meat closer to the fire than the white meat. Cover the grill and cook until an instant-read thermometer inserted into the thickest pieces of chicken registers 160°F for white meat and 165°F for dark meat, about 50 minutes.

3 cups pineapple juice, divided

2 tablespoons 3x-roasted Korean Bamboo Salt, divided

½ cup gochujang, divided

4 pounds bone-in chicken parts

Mild vegetable oil, for coating grill grate

2 tablespoons honey

1 tablespoon wasabi powder

3 tablespoons Korean black vinegar (heukcho)

1 scallion, green part only, thinly sliced

2 teaspoons finely diced red onion

1 tablespoon thinly sliced fresh cilantro leaves

1 tablespoon Toasted Sesame Salt (recipe follows)

Continued

While the chicken is cooking, in a medium saucepan over medium heat, bring the remaining 1 cup of pineapple juice, remaining 1 teaspoon of salt, remaining 6 tablespoons of gochujang, the honey, wasabi, and vinegar to a boil. Turn the heat down so the sauce simmers; simmer until lightly thickened, about 10 minutes.

About 6 minutes before the chicken is done, brush the chicken with half the sauce, turn, cover, and cook for 3 minutes. Brush with the remaining sauce, turn, cover, and cook for another 3 minutes.

Transfer the chicken to a large serving platter. Sprinkle with the scallion, red onion, and cilantro. Dust with the sesame salt and serve.

Toasted Sesame Salt

MAKES 5 TABLESPOONS

Fantastic on edamame, steamed vegetables, grilled fish, burgers, popcorn, duck fat–fried potatoes, the rim of a bloody Mary, and much more.

1 tablespoon fleur de sel

3 tablespoons sesame seeds, toasted, divided

¾ inch square dried nori

1 tablespoon delicate flake salt

Put the fleur de sel, 2 tablespoons of the sesame seeds, and the nori in a spice or coffee grinder. Grind for 30 seconds, tapping the sides a few times to knock any of the adhering mixture from the sides. Pour into a small bowl. Add the remaining 1 tablespoon of sesame seeds and the flake salt and stir with a small spoon until the salt blend is evenly coating the flake salt crystals.

KOREAN BAMBOO SALT

Korean Bamboo Salt comes in many varieties. The more times the salt is roasted, the more powerful the flavor: 1x comes off as merely a mild salt; 3x is alluringly different; 6x is hard to find, but when you do find it, you may very well want to dilute it down with another salt, because boy is it powerful: eggy, sulfuric, and intense. Which brings me to Jukyeom, also known as 9x roasted bamboo salt. *Powerful* is not the word. More like *nuclear*. This salt has actually been shown in serious, peer-reviewed medical research to lower blood pressure, ward off cancer, and more. It comes in two major types: an amethyst-colored variety and an oyster-colored variety. Each is subtly different in flavor and is reputed by some to have slightly different therapeutic properties. There are plenty of homeopath-minded cooks who advocate using 9x in cooking. I have yet to find the courage to use it on unsuspecting dinner guests.

Roasted Wings with Buffalo Salt

MAKES 4 SERVINGS

In 1964, buffalo wings got their start in Buffalo, New York, when Teressa Bellissimo deep-fried some leftover chicken wings and served them with melted butter and hot sauce. From there, hot wings have traveled the world over, picking up every flavor imaginable. Ours is classic, except we replace the sauce with blended salt. The result is dynamic. Sal de Gusano, named for the larvae found on agave roots (a Oaxacan delicacy) that are drowned in bottles of mezcal, has a hefty dose of umami, but also an incendiary flare from habanero chiles. Just the thing to make these baked hot wings take flight.

Put the vinegar in a small saucepan and boil over medium-high heat until reduced by half. Stir in the brown sugar. Remove and reserve 1 teaspoon, and toss the rest with the chicken wings. Refrigerate while the oven preheats.

Preheat the oven to 375°F.

Mix the paprika, garlic powder, cayenne, ground mustard, salt, and black pepper in a small bowl. Toss 2 tablespoons with the wings, and put the wings on a sheet pan in a single layer, evenly spaced and not touching. Roast until browned and crisp on the edges, about 45 minutes.

Combine the melted butter, the remaining 4 teaspoons of spice mixture, and the reserved 1 teaspoon of vinegar mixture in a large serving bowl. Toss the hot wings with this seasoning mixture and serve immediately.

½ cup apple cider vinegar

¼ cup packed dark brown sugar

3 pounds chicken wings, cut into sections, tips saved for another use

1 tablespoon sweet paprika

2 teaspoons garlic powder

1 teaspoon cayenne pepper

1 teaspoon ground mustard

1 teaspoon Sal de Gusano

2 teaspoons freshly ground black pepper

1 tablespoon unsalted butter, melted

> SALT BOX
>
> Fleur de Hell; Scorpion Salt; or any fiery, hot, chile-infused sea salt

Salt-Perfected Roast Chicken

MAKES 4 SERVINGS

Always salt your roast chicken from the inside out. This isn't about seasoning the bird fully. The most important role salt plays here is that it denatures the proteins of the connective tissues around the bones, developing incomparably savory chicken flavor and releasing it into the rest of meat. The cavity is the only thing you actually need to salt to roast chicken perfectly. Even after salting it generously, the chicken emerges from the oven strategically underseasoned, which leaves plenty of room to add several glorious pinches of moist, mineral-rich sel gris right before serving–bringing everything to life with a satisfyingly salt-perfected crunch.

3 ribs celery, cut into 1-inch slices

1 medium yellow onion, cut into 1-inch wedges

2 yellow potatoes, cut into 1-inch wedges

2 carrots, peeled and cut into 1-inch chunks

2 tablespoons extra-virgin olive oil, divided

6 sprigs rosemary, cut in half, divided

2 teaspoons sel gris, divided, plus more for serving

1 teaspoon cracked black peppercorns, divided, plus more for serving

1 (4-pound) chicken, visible fat removed, washed and dried

2 tablespoons dry vermouth

Preheat the oven to 425°F.

Toss the celery, onion, potatoes, and carrots with 1 tablespoon of the olive oil in a large roasting pan. Stick 4 of the rosemary pieces into the vegetables and scatter with 1½ teaspoons of the sel gris and ½ teaspoon of the cracked pepper.

Sprinkle the interior cavity of the chicken with the remaining ½ teaspoon of sel gris and ½ teaspoon of cracked pepper. Put 6 of the rosemary pieces into the cavity. Coat the outside of the chicken with the remaining 1 tablespoon of olive oil and place the chicken breast side down on top of the vegetables.

Roast for 45 minutes. Decrease the oven temperature to 400°F, and turn the chicken breast side up. It's easiest to use large tongs with one arm inserted into the chicken cavity and the other gripping the top of the chicken. Roast for 20 minutes more, or until the skin is golden brown and a thermometer inserted into the thickest part of the thigh registers 165°F.

Remove the chicken to a carving board and let rest for 5 minutes before carving. Carve the chicken and arrange in the center of a platter. Remove and discard the rosemary pieces from the chicken and roasted vegetables and, using a slotted spoon, arrange the vegetables around the chicken.

Pour off any excess fat, leaving just a film of fat over the juices on the roasting pan. Place the roasting pan on a burner and turn the heat to medium-high. Add the leaves of the remaining 2 rosemary pieces and the vermouth to the drippings in the pan. Bring to a boil, and spoon over the chicken and vegetables. Scatter more sel gris and cracked pepper over all and serve.

SALT BOX

Any French sel gris or Piran Sel Gris, Sal de Ibiza Granito, Dolce di Cervia or other medium-coarse salt like Maine Sea Salt, Oryx Desert Smoked Salt, or Antarctic Sea Salt.

Lotus-Wrapped Chicken in Salt Crust

MAKES 4 SERVINGS

Most ancient cultures with a coastline made sea salt pastes to protect meats roasting in open fires. A salt paste solidifies into a hard crust that distributes heat evenly to a roasting bird or whole fish as the salt seasons and crisps the skin. There is a long tradition of salt crust roasting in France and an even older one in China. The trick to making salt paste is starting with a powerfully moist salt, like sel gris. Most sel gris is about 13 percent seawater, moist enough to cling to itself when pressed, like packing snow into snowballs. Kosher salt won't work as well here, as it has to be moistened with tap water, which starts to dissolve it, causing it to leach its salinity into anything it touches. In this recipe, I use sel gris and give it added perfume by wrapping the chicken in fragrant dried lotus leaves.

2 cloves garlic, minced

1 inch fresh ginger, finely chopped

1 teaspoon Tsushima No Moshio

1 teaspoon crushed Sichuan peppercorns

1 (4-pound) chicken, wing tips removed, cut into 4 sections

2 tablespoons vegetable oil

2 dried lotus leaves

1 tablespoon toasted sesame oil

3 to 4 cups (2 pounds) sel gris

2 to 5 tablespoons water (optional)

2 tablespoons white shoyu soy sauce

1 tablespoon fresh lemon juice

A pinch of shio salt for accent

Preheat the oven to 400°F.

Mix the garlic, ginger, Tsushima No Moshio, and Sichuan peppercorns in a small bowl. Rub the chicken sections all over with the mixture.

Heat the vegetable oil in a large skillet over medium-high heat and brown the chicken sections as evenly as possible all around, about 2 minutes per side.

Soak the lotus leaves in a large bowl of warm water until flexible, 5 to 10 minutes. Cut the leaves in half along their center spines and lay out flat on a work surface. Put a piece of chicken at one end of each leaf. Drizzle each piece of chicken with the sesame oil, and roll each up in the lotus leaf, folding in the sides as you go, in the same way you would roll a burrito. Tie the leaves in place with cooking twine.

Press the sel gris between your fingers. It should be moist enough to stick together. If it isn't, stir in a few tablespoons of water until the salt is moist enough to cling together when firmly pressed. In a large shallow baking dish or roasting pan, make a ½-inch-thick oval of the sel gris, just large enough to hold the lotus bundles. Put the lotus-wrapped chicken pieces on the salt; it is okay if they overlap. Pack the remaining salt over the top until the lotus-wrapped chicken is completely encased. Bake for 1 hour.

Remove the chicken from the oven and let stand for 5 minutes. Mix the shoyu soy sauce and lemon juice in a small bowl.

Break the salt crust with a mallet. Serve a lotus-wrapped chicken bundle to each person. Snip the string tying the lotus leaves. Unfold the leaves, drizzle some of the lemon-shoyu mixture over each serving, and a sprinkling of more shio; eat the chicken from its leaf wrapper.

Turkey Wanderlust

MAKES 4 SERVINGS

If you don't know about turkey London broil, it's probably because you never cared. It's nothing more than a butterflied boneless turkey breast, like beef London broil. But this turkey cut is an enthusiastic companion to all sorts of marinades and seasoning rubs—and it cooks in less than 10 minutes. To celebrate its underappreciated versatility, we have teamed it with four globally inspired rubs, each inspired and powered by a distinctive craft salt. Choose your weapon.

SMOKED ORANGE ANISE RUB

1 tablespoon finely grated orange zest

1 tablespoon smoked salt (such as hickory, alder, or cherry)

1 tablespoon demerara sugar

2 teaspoons smoked ground black pepper

2 teaspoons ground anise seeds

MOROCCAN SALT RUB

1 tablespoon ground thyme

1 tablespoon demerara sugar

1 teaspoon ground cinnamon

1 teaspoon any Mediterranean sea salt (such as Cuor di Trapani Sea Salt or Trapani e Marsala Sea Salt)

1 teaspoon ground coriander

½ teaspoon coarsely ground black pepper

½ teaspoon finely grated lemon zest

½ teaspoon ground turmeric

SESAME SICHUAN SALT RUB

2 tablespoons cracked Sichuan peppercorns

1 tablespoon sesame seeds, toasted

1 tablespoon shio (such as Full Moon Shio for mineral brightness or Tsushima No Moshio for umami)

1 teaspoon cracked black pepper

½ teaspoon ground ginger

ROSE SALT CHIMICHURRI RUB

⅓ cup finely chopped fresh flat-leaf parsley

1 clove garlic, minced

1 tablespoon grated yellow onion

1 teaspoon finely ground rock salt (such as Persian Blue Salt for mild sweetness or Himalayan Pink Salt for bold saltiness)

½ teaspoon dried marjoram

¼ teaspoon freshly ground black pepper

¼ teaspoon red pepper flakes

2 pounds boneless turkey breast, cut for London broil, or turkey tenders

1 recipe salt rub of choice

1 tablespoon olive oil

To make the rub of your choice, combine all of the ingredients in a small bowl.

To prepare the turkey, rub it with your selected rub and drizzle with the oil. Set aside for 15 minutes.

Preheat a grill or broiler to medium-high direct heat.

If grilling, clean the grill grate with a grill scraper. If broiling, put the turkey on a broiler pan. Grill or broil the turkey until browned and resilient to the touch, about 4 minutes per side. An instant-read thermometer inserted into one end should register 160°F. Transfer to a carving board and rest for 5 to 10 minutes before slicing against the grain.

Note: These rubs can be used on a variety of meats. Consider multiplying any or all of the recipes above and keep any extra in reserve for a quick and easy roasted or grilled dinner. Each can be stored in the refrigerator in a tightly closed jar for up to 2 weeks.

Chicken Roulade Fireworks

MAKES 4 SERVINGS

I once knew a French woman who ate only chicken breast. Dropping by her apartment, about the size of a spacious motel bathroom, was always an emotionally confusing experience. The dread of the impossibly cluttered, unkempt apartment was matched by the anticipation of her inevitably delicious cooking. I was never a chicken lover, but to her it was a blank canvas on which to paint layers of color, texture, and flavor. Here we spiral pounded breast with layers of pungent dark greens, tangy goat cheese, flaming red peppers, and startling black flake salt. The roulades are coated with a thin glaze of pesto that crusts and caramelizes in the frying pan, coating the Technicolor rolls with a crunchy lacquer tasty enough to lure visitors to any home.

Place each chicken breast between two sheets of waxed paper or plastic wrap, smooth side down. Pound with the flat side of a mallet or a heavy skillet to an even ¼-inch thickness, being careful not to tear the meat.

Sprinkle each piece of chicken with the fleur de sel and pepper. Then divide and spread on the goat cheese, leaving a ¼-inch border around the edges. Top with one-quarter of the arugula, a few roasted peppers, some scallions, and some flake salt. Roll up jelly-roll style from a short side, pushing in the sides as you roll, to enclose the filling. Secure with toothpicks or skewers. Brush the pesto over the surface of each piece of chicken. To make ahead, cover and refrigerate for up to 8 hours. Remove from the refrigerator 1 hour before cooking.

Heat a large skillet over medium heat. Add the oil and sauté the chicken rolls until browned on all sides, about 4 minutes per side, 16 minutes total. When done, the rolls will be browned and feel firm when gently squeezed. Remove the toothpicks and slice crosswise on a slight diagonal to reveal the filling. Shingle the slices on plates and sprinkle with a few more flake salt crystals.

4 boneless skinless chicken breast halves, about 1½ pounds total

½ teaspoon fleur de sel or shio

¼ teaspoon freshly ground black pepper

6 ounces soft goat cheese

1 packed cup baby arugula

¾ cup roasted red bell peppers, store-bought or homemade, drained

1 small scallion, finely chopped

2 teaspoons Black Diamond Flake Salt, plus more for garnish

¼ cup basil pesto, store-bought or homemade

1 tablespoon olive oil

SALT BOX

Icelandic Flake Salt, Kilauea Onyx Sea Salt, Black Lava Salt

Fleur de Hell Fried Chicken

MAKES 4 SERVINGS

This numbingly salty, fiery, fragrant fried chicken is proof that Heaven orders its takeout from the underworld. The secret is the combination in my own flaming salt, which I call Fleur de Hell—a mixture of fleur de sel and Indian bhut jolokia (ghost chiles), and Sichuan peppercorns. Sichuan peppercorns, actually the dried hulls of berries, have nothing to do with black, white, or green peppercorns. They are barely spicy hot but are floral, mentholated, a little sweet, and dramatically numbing. Sichuan pepper anesthetizes the palate in a magical way, blurring its sensations so that it can take an insane amount of salty prickles and hot chile burn without experiencing pain. Your taste buds will thank you, even if they have to travel through hell and back.

1½ cups buttermilk

5 teaspoons Fleur de Hell,
    divided

3 cloves garlic, minced

½ cup coarsely chopped fresh
    herbs (such as marjoram,
    rosemary, thyme, sage, flat-leaf
    parsley, etc.)

3 pounds boneless skinless
    chicken pieces

2 teaspoons freshly ground black
    pepper

1 teaspoon crushed Sichuan
    peppercorns

1 teaspoon ground cayenne
    pepper

½ teaspoon ground fiery chile
    (such as ghost, bird,
    or habanero)

1 large egg, beaten

1½ cups all-purpose flour

Vegetable oil, for frying

3 whole dried red chiles (such as
    cayenne)

Mix the buttermilk, 3 teaspoons of the Fleur de Hell, garlic, and herbs in a small bowl. Put the chicken in a gallon-size resealable plastic bag and pour in 1 cup of the buttermilk mixture. Massage to make sure all of the chicken is coated. Squeeze out any excess air and seal tight. Refrigerate for at least 2 hours. If it is convenient, you can allow the chicken to marinate in the buttermilk for as long as 24 hours. Refrigerate the remaining ½ cup of buttermilk mixture in a separate container.

Meanwhile, mix the remaining 2 teaspoons of Fleur de Hell, black pepper, Sichuan pepper, cayenne, and fiery chile; store in a tightly closed container for up to 1 month.

Mix the reserved ½ cup buttermilk mixture and egg in a pie plate; set aside.

Mix the flour and half the spice mixture in another pie plate or on a sheet of aluminum foil.

Remove the chicken from the bag and wipe off any milk mixture clinging to the chicken. Discard the liquid in the bag.

Dredge the chicken in the flour mixture and pat off any excess. There should just be enough flour on the surface of the chicken to make the surface dry. Roll the floured chicken in the buttermilk-egg mixture, and dredge in the flour again, making sure it is well coated. Place on a rack set over a sheet pan to dry while the oil heats.

Heat ¾ inch oil in a deep heavy skillet large enough to hold the chicken without crowding until it registers 350°F on a deep-fry thermometer. Decrease the heat to medium to keep the oil temperature steady. Add the whole chiles to the oil.

Fry the chicken pieces for 8 to 10 minutes, until golden brown and a thermometer inserted in the center of a big piece reads 165°F. Drain on paper towels; dust with the remaining spice mixture and serve immediately.

SALT BOX

Scorpion Salt or any intense, chile-infused craft salt will do. For a less spicy recipe, substitute glitter-fire salt like Saltwest Naturals Sea Salt or San Juan Island Sea Salt.

House-Cured Chicken Sausage

MAKES 6 TO 8 SERVINGS

Usually when we cook with salt, our end goal is to slap some sense into your taste buds, and set them quivering with the play between minerality and food, but when curing, the role of salt minerals become less sensorial and more chemical, virtually subatomic. The purpose of the salt in this recipe is to reinvent the meat and, through that, your taste sensations. Curing changes the character of raw meat from deep inside (see Curing Salts, opposite), producing protein that is more tangy than savory, more sweet and salty than rich and unctuous. When properly done, the salt in a cure should disappear, making it nearly impossible for your palate to parse exactly where the salt leaves off and the cured meat begins.

1 pound boneless skin-on chicken breast, cut into 1-inch pieces

2 pounds boneless skin-on chicken thighs, cut into 1-inch pieces

2 teaspoons finely ground traditional salt

½ teaspoon Prague Powder #1

2 teaspoons dried rubbed sage

1 teaspoon freshly ground black pepper

½ teaspoon ground nutmeg

½ teaspoon red pepper flakes

½ cup dried nonfat milk powder

1 large yellow onion, coarsely shredded

½ cup chopped dried apples

Spread the chicken pieces out on a sheet pan and freeze until firm but not solid, about 20 minutes.

Mix both the salts in a large bowl. Add the sage, pepper, nutmeg, pepper flakes, and milk powder and mix thoroughly.

Run the chicken through the medium plate of a meat grinder, and toss well with the spice mixture, onion, and apples. Grind the mixture one more time through the medium plate.

Refrigerate, tightly covered, for 24 to 48 hours to allow the meat to cure.

Form into 2-ounce patties (about ½ inch thick and 2½ inches in diameter) and sauté over medium-high heat until cooked through, about 5 minutes per side. The raw sausages can be stored tightly covered in the refrigerator for up to 3 days.

CURING SALTS

Curing means to preserve something in salt. Salt reduces the water activity in the meat, inhibiting the growth of harmful bacteria. It also improves taste, unraveling proteins in the muscle fiber, improving its texture, and creating more flavor-available amino acids. In the case of fermented meats, salt also gives desirable bacteria like *Lactobacillus plantarum* and *Pediococcus acidilactici* time to grow, increasing acidity and creating a formidable, lasting barrier to the growth of undesired bacteria. Curing also creates an environment for *Micrococcus* bacteria that further improve flavor.

Because all salt is antibacterial, all salt preserves. But there are special kinds of salt called "curing salts" that are especially effective against *Clostridium botulinum*, the bacteria that produces the deadly toxin botulism. *Botulinum* only grow in an oxygen-deprived environment, such as at the center of large dense meats like whole hams and salamis. Sodium nitrite and sodium nitrate are the main curing salts today, replacing more traditional curing salts like saltpeter (potassium nitrate).

Prague Powder #1 (also called Pink Salt, Instacure #1, DQ Cure #1, and sometimes just "curing salt" for short) contains regular sodium chloride and 6.25 percent sodium nitrite. This premixed blend of regular salt and nitrite salt is specially formulated for short curing times (days), such as when making pâtés, bacon, unfermented sausage, pastrami, and fish.

Prague Powder #2 contains 6.25 percent sodium nitrite plus 4 percent sodium nitrate. It is used in dry-cured, fermented meats like dry salamis, prosciutto, and other hams. The nitrate is sort of time-delayed nitrite, as bacteria like *Staphylococcus carnosus* and *Staphylococcus xylosus* will convert all nitrate entirely into nitrite by the time the cure is complete. Properly cured meats should contain no nitrate at all.

Nitrites don't just kill bacteria, they also set the red-pigmented myoglobin in meat, giving cured meat its attractive color and the delicious tang that any lover of traditional sausage craves. This is not to say that all cures require curing salt. Curing salt is actually forbidden in traditional prosciutto and serrano hams. Instead, producers use regular salt only and, after aging, poke a long toothpick made of horse bone into the arteries and bones of the ham and then smell it to determine if botulism is present. This nitrite-free tradition yields formidably tasty ham but results in waste and is therefore costly.

Some people are concerned that nitrites can break down into nitrosamines that may cause gastric cancer. There is scant hard evidence to back the fear, and the American National Research Council of the National Academy of Sciences maintains that the safety benefits of nitrites far outweigh any risks. Nitrates are a naturally occurring substance, and it is speculated that diets high in nitrate-rich foods promote vascular health, dilating blood vessels and lowering blood pressure. Nitrate was even used in a 7th-century Chinese medical prescription to treat angina.

Dry-Brined Roast Turkey with Cider Jus

MAKES 15 SERVINGS

Salting and slow roasting solves all of life's problems—if you're a roast turkey. The slow roasting makes for moist, perfectly done turkey. The salting crisps the skin as surely as baking your bird in an inferno. Salt draws protein-rich juices from under the skin to the surface, where the moisture evaporates and the proteins crisp, producing a delicious bronzed crust. Rubs are generally made with fine salt for even distribution. However, fine salt tends to dry turkey too much; coarse sel gris does a great job of drawing protein-filled juices to the skin without drying out the breast meat, and the coarse crystals deliver the celebratory salty zing that every roast turkey dreams of.

1 (15-pound) fresh turkey

3 tablespoons coarse sea salt (such as sel gris), plus more for garnish

1 tablespoon coarsely ground black pepper

1 tablespoon olive oil

4 cups apple cider

½ teaspoon each dried thyme, dried sage, and crushed dried rosemary

SALT BOX

Bulls Bay Charleston Sea Salt, Maine Sea Salt, Yellowstone Natural Salt, Wellfleet Sea Salt, Bora Bora Sea Salt

Pat the turkey dry with paper towels and rub it all over with the salt and pepper. Refrigerate uncovered for 24 hours. During that time, the surface of the turkey will become visibly dry and the skin will tighten.

Take the turkey out of the refrigerator 1 hour before you want to start roasting. Preheat the oven to 450°F.

Put the turkey on a rack set in a large roasting pan. Drizzle the oil over the top. Roast for 1 hour. Decrease the oven temperature to 170°F; add the cider and herbs to the roasting pan and continue roasting until an instant-read thermometer inserted into the thickest part of a thigh (without touching bone) reads 170°F, about 12 hours.

Transfer the turkey to a carving board. Rest at room temperature for 15 minutes. Meanwhile, skim the fat from the surface of the liquid in the pan. Put the roasting pan on the stovetop and bring the drippings to a boil over high heat. Reduce until thickened enough to coat a spoon, about 10 minutes. Taste for seasoning and adjust as needed. Carve the turkey, sprinkle with more salt, and serve with the cider pan juices.

Quail on the Rocks

MAKES 4 SERVINGS

Salt is a mineral that turns into rock under pressure. Like all rocks, salt absorbs heat and will conduct it to any food that is placed on it. Cooking on Himalayan Pink Salt blocks has become hugely fashionable (check out my cookbook *Salt Block Cooking*), and this recipe is a raucously aromatic reason to do just that. Chunks of Himalayan Pink Salt are heated in a roasting pan with aromatic spices. You can use rough-cut rocks, coarse Himalayan Pink Salt, or broken-up salt blocks. Then boneless quail are placed on the hot rocks and roasted, wafting in the aroma of roasting spices and subtly seasoned from being in contact with the hot salt.

Preheat the oven to 400°F.

Mix the salt rocks, 4 cinnamon sticks, 12 peppercorns, red pepper flakes, and 4 star anise in a large roasting pan. Heat in the oven for 30 minutes, until the salt is hot and the spices are aromatic.

Meanwhile, put the remaining 2 cinnamon sticks, 6 peppercorns, 1 star anise, sherry, and sherry vinegar in a small saucepan and boil over medium-high heat until thickened and reduced to about ⅓ cup. Strain and reserve.

Remove the pan of hot salt and place the quail breast-side up on the hot salt rocks. Return to the oven and roast until the skin on the quail has browned and the meat is firm to the touch, about 15 minutes. Brush with half of the spiced sherry glaze and roast for 3 more minutes to set the glaze.

Lift the quail from the salt and serve drizzled with the remaining glaze.

1 pound Himalayan Pink Salt rocks, coarse salt, or broken salt blocks

6 cinnamon sticks, smashed with a hammer, divided

18 black peppercorns, smashed with a hammer, divided

Big pinch of red pepper flakes

5 star anise, broken into pieces, divided

¾ cup dry sherry

¼ cup sherry vinegar

8 (¼-pound) semi-boneless quail

SALT BOX

If you can't find small rocks or coarse pebbles of rock salt, large rocks or even unwanted Himalayan Pink Salt blocks can be broken up with a hammer into marble-sized chunks.

CHAPTER 3

SEAFOOD

Seafood tastes good for a reason. Fish, shellfish, and cephalopods live in salt, and their salty lifestyle radically affects their flavor. Ocean fish that swallow salty water need to develop ways to maintain the mineral balance in their bodily fluids. Saltwater is about 3.5 percent mineral salts by weight, but the optimal level of dissolved mineral salts in animal cells is less than 1 percent. Sea creatures balance the salinity of ocean water by filling their cells with amines and amino acids, the building blocks of proteins. The amino acid glycine is quite sweet, and glutamic acid is the very essence of umami. The flesh of ocean fish has the same salinity as beef or pork, but three to ten times more free amino acids—that means flavor. Also, because of their high protein levels, seafood can accept a good deal of salting without becoming salty. Besides seasoning, there are two key ways to salt fish and shellfish.

1. Sprinkling some salt on the skin of a fish before cooking will remove moisture and increase crispness. The salt draws moisture to the surface, where it evaporates. The best approach is to salt the skin of a fillet and let it sit uncovered on a plate, skin side up, for about an hour in the refrigerator before cooking. Whole fish need to be set on a rack over a sheet pan to let air circulate on all sides. This is done because fish skin is rich in collagen, which, when moistened, turns into gelatin—and we're all familiar with the wiggly consistency of warm gelatin. If you want superbly crisp skin, salt it beforehand. Steaks or skinless fillets need not be salted in advance—leaving you free to salt it with a delicate, complementary finishing salt at the table.

2. Salting seafood and shellfish will "cook" seafood, causing proteins to unravel and firm up in much the same way as heat does. Packing salt on the surface of fish causes moisture to pass out of the cells via osmosis, concentrating its flavor. When making gravlax or some kinds of ceviche, this is the technique that is used. Serving sashimi on a salt bock is another; the salted side of the fish pales, takes on firmness, and develops richer, more savory flavor.

Fish owe the delicacy of their flesh to the fact that they live in water, and water is denser than air; a life swimming weightlessly in salty seawater spares them the sturdy skeletons and tough muscles of land animals. Salt brings a satisfying terrestrial firmness to the tenderness of fish.

			FISH					SHELLFISH				
			roasted	grilled	fried	raw	steamed	roasted	grilled	fried	raw	steamed
SALTS	fleur de sel		X	X	X	X		X	X	X		
	sel gris			X						X	X	
	flake	fine	X	X	X	X		X	X	X	X	
		coarse	X	X								
	traditional	fine	X	X	X	X	X	X	X		X	X
		coarse		X								
	shio		X	X	X	X	X	X	X	X	X	X
	rock	fine			X		X	X				X
		coarse	X	X					X			
		block	X	X		X			X		X	
	infused	smoked	X			X		X	X			
		flavored	X	X		X			X	X		

Tuna Steaks with Thai Steak Salt

MAKES 4 SERVINGS

Tuna is the prime rib of seafood. More akin to beef in size, color, heartiness, and meatiness than it is to any other sea life, it is no wonder we always eat tuna as steaks. The Thai spice paste that cloaks the tuna in this recipe is worthy of all its oceanic machismo. Its base is Sal de Gusano, a brick-red salt blend that includes ground Gusano larvae, of mezcal fame, and a good jolt of pasilla and arbol chiles. In Thai tradition, the salt is mixed with toasted rice powder, which absorbs moisture from the fish and forms a solid crust that crisps as the tuna steak sears.

Heat a heavy skillet over medium heat for 3 minutes. Add the rice and stir until the rice has colored to the hue of brown rice, about 10 minutes. Do not rush the process; the rice can easily burn. Cool to room temperature, and grind to a powder in a spice grinder or mortar and pestle. Store in a closed container at room temperature for up to 1 week.

Mix 2 teaspoons of the Sal de Gusano, 2 tablespoons of the toasted rice powder, the sugar, and basil in a small bowl. Rub all over the tuna steaks and set aside for 10 minutes.

While the tuna rests, mix the lime juice, fish sauce, cilantro, scallion, remaining 1 teaspoon of Sal de Gusano, and 1 tablespoon toasted rice powder in a small bowl; set aside.

Heat a large, heavy skillet, preferably cast iron, over high heat for 5 minutes. It should be white-hot. Coat the tuna steaks with the sesame oil and brown the steaks until charred on the outside but still raw inside, about 2 minutes per side.

Slice against the grain into ⅜-inch-thick slices. Shingle on a serving platter. Drizzle with the reserved salted lime sauce and sprinkle with the sesame seeds.

¼ cup glutinous rice

1 tablespoon Sal de Gusano, divided

1 teaspoon sugar

1 teaspoon dried basil

1¾ pounds tuna steaks, cut 2 inches thick

⅓ cup fresh lime juice

⅓ cup Thai fish sauce

2 tablespoons chopped fresh cilantro

1 scallion, finely chopped

1 tablespoon toasted sesame oil

2 tablespoons sesame seeds, toasted

SALT BOX

If Sal de Gusano is not on hand, just use any salt and add a pinch of hot ground chiles of choice.

Shio Crust Whole Grilled Fish

MAKES 2 SERVINGS

The fire-evaporated salts of Japan (shio) are prized for their delicate, silken crystal structure, but next to the tender fibers of a smacking fresh snapper or bass, shio comes off brazenly bold. In this recipe, the shio is Moshio, a salt evaporated from seaweed brine that has pronounced umami tastes. Mix the Moshio with kelp flakes and Sichuan peppercorns for an extra goose of umami. Sichuan pepper is only mildly peppery, but it is markedly anesthetizing. Your comfortably numb tongue will taste sparks of shio through a mist of seafood savor.

1 (1 to 2-pound) whole white-fleshed saltwater fish (such as red snapper or black bass), gutted, scaled, fins trimmed

1 tablespoon Tsushima No Moshio

1 teaspoon crushed Sichuan peppercorns

1 teaspoon dried kelp flakes

1 tablespoon peanut oil

Mild vegetable oil, for coating grill screen

Finely grated zest and juice of 1 lime

2 tablespoons finely chopped fresh cilantro

SALT BOX

Shinkai Deep Sea Salt, Jigen No Moshio, Full Moon Shio, Bitterman's Fine Traditional Sea Salt, Vancouver Island Sea Salt, San Juan Island Sea Salt

---

Scrape the dull side of a knife against the skin of the fish, running from tail to head, to remove any excess moisture and remaining scales. Cut 3 or 4 diagonal slices through the flesh of the fish on each side down to the bone.

Mix the Tsushima No Moshio, Sichuan pepper, and kelp in a small bowl. Season the fish inside and out with the salt mixture. Set on a rack perched on a plate and refrigerate for 1 hour.

Preheat the grill for direct medium heat (350° to 400°F). Set a grill screen over the fire.

Rub the outside of the fish with the peanut oil. Oil the grill screen liberally with vegetable oil and put the fish on the screen. Cover the grill and cook until browned all over and an instant-read thermometer inserted into the thickest part of the fish registers 130°F, 7 to 8 minutes per side. If your grill has a temperature gauge, it should stay around 375°F.

Transfer the fish to a serving platter. Drizzle the fish with the lime juice and scatter the lime zest and cilantro over the top. Lift the fish fillets from the bones to serve.

Mixed Fish Ceviche on Crispy Salted Tortilla Chips

MAKES 6 SERVINGS

Ceviche, the Latin method of "cooking" seafood in acidic citrus juice, is not unlike gravlax, the Nordic method of "cooking" salmon in salt. Both techniques denature the protein and draw moisture from the raw seafood, causing it to become, firmer, denser, more opaque, and—need I say—more flavorful. In this Latino-Norse hybrid recipe, we take inspiration from both traditions and add a little boiling saltwater. Oaxaca's famed savory, salty, spicy condiment Sal de Gusano brings the recipe back home to its native territory. The result is a descant of perfectly cooked shellfish and ocean fish, syncopated with crisp shards of celery and red onion, a peppering of fresh ginger, and cilantro. Scoop it up with decadently salted homemade tortilla chips.

Big pinch fine sea salt

¼ pound medium (26–30 count) shrimp, shelled and deveined

6 sea scallops, trimmed and quartered

2 small squid, cleaned, bodies cut in ½-inch rings, tentacles left whole

½ pound skinless red snapper fillet, cut into ½-inch pieces

¼ pound skinless wild salmon fillet, cut into ½-inch pieces

6 teaspoons Flor de Sal de Manzanillo

1 tablespoon chopped fresh ginger

1 rib celery, finely chopped

Finely grated zest of 3 limes

Juice of 6 limes

¼ cup chopped fresh cilantro

½ red onion, finely chopped

Freshly ground black pepper

¾ cup corn oil

6 corn tortillas, left out overnight to harden

1 teaspoon Sal de Gusano

Continued

SALT BOX

Ceviche: **Fleur de Hell or any chile-infused sea salt, or take a different tack with Taha'a Vanilla or Lemon Flake Salt.**

Chips: **Bitterman's Fleur de Sel, Fleur de Sel de l'Île de Noirmoutier, El Salvador Fleur de Sel, Flor de Sal do Algarve, Flos Salis, Fleur de Sel de Camargue, or finely ground traditional salt like Muối Biển.**

Bring 2 quarts of water to a boil. Add the salt, shrimp, scallops, and squid. Stir to distribute everything, remove from the heat, and cover. Wait 2 minutes, and then drain the seafood. Toss with the snapper, salmon, 1 teaspoon of flor de sal, ginger, celery, and lime zest. Refrigerate for 30 minutes.

Add the lime juice, stir, and refrigerate for 2 hours, stirring several times, until the snapper no longer looks raw. Stir in the cilantro, onion, and pepper.

To make the tortilla crisps, heat the oil to 375°F in a deep skillet. Cut each tortilla into 6 wedges, and fry in batches of 12, without crowding the pan, until the chips are lightly toasted and firm. Use tongs to transfer to paper towels to drain. Sprinkle with the remaining 5 teaspoons of flor de sal, dividing it among the batches of chips. Repeat with the remaining tortillas.

Sprinkle the ceviche with a generous pinch of Sal de Gusano and serve with the chips.

Chilled Shrimp with Cocktail Salt

MAKES 4 SERVINGS

Being gourmet was so much easier last century. All you needed were a few free-ranging Buick-size shrimp and a jar of cocktail sauce. Farmed shrimp aren't what their free-ranging predecessors were, and nowadays, well, there's no sugar-coating the cold ooze of ketchup and horseradish. We modernize and intensify the flavor profile of shrimp cocktail by switching from cocktail sauce to cocktail salt, a mixture of spiced fleur de sel, wasabi powder (Japanese horseradish), hot paprika (dried hot chiles), and tomato powder (a versatile flavoring that is 100 percent natural). This powderized, Asian-influenced, salt-fueled version of a cocktail sauce hits your mouth like a school of flaming piranha that's definitely hungry for shrimp.

Bring 2 quarts of water to a boil. Add the traditional salt and return to a boil. Add the shrimp, stir, cover, and remove from the heat. Wait 2 minutes and then drain the shrimp.

Mix the tomato powder, wasabi powder, hot pepper salt, and paprika, and toss with the warm shrimp. Chill.

Crunch the lemon salt over the top and serve with the lemon wedges.

1 tablespoon traditional salt

1 pound jumbo (16–20 count) shrimp, shells removed except for tail, deveined

2 teaspoons tomato powder

1½ teaspoons wasabi powder

1 teaspoon hot pepper salt (such as Fleur de Hell)

1 teaspoon hot paprika

1 teaspoon Lemon Flake Salt

1 lemon, cut into 4 wedges

> ## SALT BOX
>
> Any spicy chile-infused salt will do. The best alternative to the lemon salt is to take a totally different tack with the faintly acidic, aromatic crystals of Pinot Noir Sea Salt. Alternately, any plain coarse flake salt, such as Achill Island Sea Salt, Cornish Flake Sea Salt, Maldon Sea Salt, Hana Flake Salt, Jacobsen Flake, Cyprus Silver Flake Sea Salt, or Halen Môn Silver Flake Sea Salt will do.

Roasted Lobster with Vanilla Salt and Smoky Scotch Butter

MAKES 2 SERVINGS

Roasting on a bed of fragrant vanilla and maple-smoked salts infuses lobster with lovely aromas of both tropical paradise and northern Atlantic ruggedness. The collision of these remote lands on your palate is fantastic. Dipping each bite in a butter bath of syrupy, smoky Scotch doesn't hurt either. One important tip: The way you kill a lobster affects the texture and flavor of its meat dramatically. Sorry to bring it up. If a lobster experiences stress shortly before dying, glycogen stores in its muscles (part of what makes its meat taste sweet) get used up and the resulting cooked lobster has much less flavor than one that dies relaxed. That's why the recipe tells you to stroke the lobsters' swimmerets along the underside of the body. I know it feels a bit kinky, but you will see the lobster visibly relax each time you touch its little flippers. And that single act of kindness makes all the difference.

2 (1¼ to 1½-pound) live lobsters

2 tablespoons Taha'a Vanilla Salt, divided

2 tablespoons Sugar Maple Smoked Sea Salt, divided

1 tablespoon olive oil

4 tablespoons unsalted butter, divided

1 shallot, finely chopped

¼ cup smoky Scotch (preferably Laphroaig 10-year)

½ teaspoon freshly ground black pepper

Place a roasting pan large enough to hold the lobsters in an oven and preheat the oven to 450°F.

One at a time, sedate the lobsters by stroking their swimmerets from the tail toward the head; the lobsters should visibly relax. Put them on their bellies, laying the tail section out flat. To kill them, stab them right behind the head, in the seam where the two shells meet. Wiggle the knife back and forth a bit to make sure you have severed the brain from the nerve ganglia. Crack the claws using the back side of a large knife or a hammer.

Sprinkle 5 teaspoons vanilla salt and 2½ teaspoons smoked salt in the bottom of the hot roasting pan. Put the lobsters on top and drizzle with the olive oil. Roast until red, about 15 minutes. Cool for 10 minutes, or until cool enough to handle.

Continued

SALT BOX

DIY Vanilla Salt: **If no ready-made vanilla salt is on hand, slit a vanilla pod and scrape the seeds into 2 tablespoons of any coarse, moist sea salt, such as sel gris. Or bring some of the briny American Northeast to the table with Maine Sea Salt, Eggemoggin Reach Salt, North Fork Sea Salt, or Outer Banks Sea Salt.**

While the lobsters are resting, melt 1 tablespoon of butter in a small skillet over medium heat. Add the shallot and sauté until translucent, about 3 minutes. Add the Scotch and reduce by half. Decrease the heat to low and swirl in the remaining 3 tablespoons of butter. Season with the remaining 1 teaspoon vanilla salt, remaining ½ teaspoon smoked salt, and pepper.

Serve the lobsters with shellfish crackers (or pliers) to disassemble the shells and small forks to help get to the meat. Serve the Scotch butter on the side for dipping.

Raw Oysters in a Shallot Sea

MAKES 4 SMALL OR 2 LARGE SERVINGS

The effect of salt on raw oysters is immediate. Returning them to the brine from which they came, the oysters perk up and plump as soon as the salt crystals make contact. Salt at the very last moment. You want to salt and gulp, salt and gulp. With oysters, the salt of choice is Shinkai Deep Sea, for its moist, delicate crystal and assertive minerality.

Combine the vermouth and shallots in a medium skillet. Boil over high heat until the liquid is reduced by half. Remove from the heat, stir in the vinegar, and set aside to cool while you prepare the oysters.

Put the oysters on a rimmed sheet pan and freeze for about 10 minutes, which will make them easier to open. To open, cover your nondominant hand with a folded towel or protective glove and hold the oyster, flat side up, in that hand. With your other hand, press a solid, dull knife (such as an oyster knife) between the hinged ends of the shells to pop the shells apart. Or use the pointed end of a beer can opener in the hinge and pry it open. Run a knife along the inside of the top shell to cut the meat from the shell, and then remove the top shell. Run the knife under the oyster to detach it from the bottom shell, but leave the oyster nestled in the shell. The liquor from fresh oysters should be clear. Pick out any shards of shell that might have broken loose during shucking.

Add the peppercorns to the shallot mixture.

Arrange the oysters on the chilled salt block. Spoon enough of the shallot mixture onto each oyster to fill the shell. Top each with a small pile of Shinkai salt. Slide an oyster, salt, and sauce from the shell into your mouth. Repeat with the remaining oysters.

½ cup dry vermouth

2 medium shallots, minced

1 tablespoon red wine vinegar

12 briny oysters (such as Totten, Kumamoto, or Olympia from the West Coast, or Pemaquid, Blue Point, or Belon from the East Coast), shells scrubbed

1 teaspoon cracked black peppercorns

Salt block or platter, chilled, for serving

Several pinches Shinkai Deep Sea Salt

SALT BOX

Full Moon Shio, Jigen No Moshio, or another superfine shio is ideal, but finely ground mineral-laden traditional salts like Popohaku Opal Sea Salt, Cuor di Trapani Sea Salt, and Sel Marin de Noirmoutier are options.

CHAPTER 4

EGGS AND DAIRY

M ost anything edible benefits from salt, but eggs require it. There is something about the blandness of an egg (even the word *albumen* sounds unexciting) that demands salt. Yet if I were stranded on that hypothetical desert island that everyone gets hypothetically stranded on, and I only had one food to eat for the rest of eternity, it might be eggs because of how dang good they would taste with all that beautiful sea salt I'd be making from the surrounding waters.

Both salt and eggs are ionic, which makes them interact dramatically, allowing you to employ salt to influence the finished textures and cooking temperatures of egg dishes in myriad ways.

1. Salt added to raw egg begins to denature its protein on contact, allowing you to play with the finished cooked texture more profoundly. The result is softer, more tender cooked eggs. It takes just takes a pinch to get the desired chemical reaction with the protein in raw eggs. So it's always advisable to save the bulk of your salt for finishing to achieve maximum flavor and texture.

2. There is one instance when salt should not be used with eggs: when making a foam of beaten egg whites. Salt inhibits the formation of peaks when beating egg whites and diminishes the stability of an egg foam. When beating egg whites, you are trying to encourage the protein strands to tangle together and form a structure that is firm enough to hold a shape. Dissolving salt in the egg whites too early makes it harder for the egg proteins to bond with one another and in the long run decreases the number of protein-to-protein bonds, weakening the overall structure. It is therefore preferable to salt the other components of dishes like soufflés and sponge cakes, rather than the foam itself. Note that this advice is contrary to the instructions of many recipes.

3. Salt eggs for scrambling or custards minimally when raw to encourage soft coagulation, but no matter what salt you add to an egg recipe before cooking, make sure you salt the finished dish liberally. As I said before, eggs demand salting. It's difficult to overdo it.

| | | | EGGS | | | | DAIRY | | |
			boiled	fried	quiche	custard	soufflé	cheese	ice cream
SALTS	fleur de sel		X	X	X	X	X	X	X
	sel gris				X			X	X
	flake	fine	X	X	X	X	X	X	
		coarse			X		X	X	X
	traditional	fine	X	X			X		
		coarse							X
	shio					X	X	X	
	rock	fine	X	X	X				
		coarse							
		block		X	X			X	X
	infused	smoked	X	X	X		X	X	X
		flavored	X	X	X		X	X	X

Deviled Eggs, Seven Salts

MAKES 5 SERVINGS

In a world of numerous egg dishes (the 100 folds of a chef's toque are said to represent the number of ways to prepare an egg), deviling is on its own continent. I know this because my sons, who can take or leave any rendition of breakfast eggs—fried, scrambled, omelet, you name it—can devour a dozen deviled eggs each as if they were potato chips. I think the only reason my kids look forward to Easter is for the eggs. Deviling is another name for spicing, and these poppers can handle any degree of aggressive seasoning you throw at them. Ours are mild compared to many, but not so when it comes to salting. Each one sports its own salt: fleur de sel, red, black, smoked, rock, flaked, and flavored. I say this makes five servings, but in my home it really only makes one.

Place the eggs in a medium saucepan and add enough water to cover. Set over medium-high heat, cover, and bring to a boil. Turn down to a simmer and simmer for 2 minutes. Remove from the heat and let sit for 12 minutes. Drain. Run under cold water until the eggs feel cool to the touch.

Crack the shells and peel carefully under cold running water. Dry the peeled eggs with paper towels. Cut the eggs in half lengthwise, transferring the yolks to a bowl. Put the whites cut-side up on a serving platter.

Mash the yolks with a fork and mix in the mayonnaise, vinegar, mustard, pepper, and fine sea salt. Mound the yolk mixture in the hollows of the egg whites, and sprinkle each egg (2 halves) with a different finishing salt. Serve immediately, or chill for up to 24 hours. If holding in the refrigerator, add the finishing salts just before serving.

7 large or extra-large eggs

¼ cup mayonnaise

1 teaspoon apple cider vinegar

1 teaspoon brown mustard

½ teaspoon freshly ground white pepper

½ teaspoon fine sea salt

2 pinches each finishing salt: fleur de sel of choice, Kala Namak or other sulfuric salt of choice, red salt of choice, black salt of choice, smoked salt of choice, rock salt of choice, and white flake salt of choice

Salt-Poached Eggs on Greens with Salt-Cured Chiles

MAKES 4 SERVINGS

This brightly hued, multidimensional recipe is both a delicious chemical treatise and a testament to global culinary wisdom: The ionic ability of salt on coagulating egg protein shapes the poached eggs into perfect rounds (a Sicilian trick), and salt's preservative abilities ensure that only probiotic bacteria reproduce in the salt-cured pickled peppers (renowned from Germany to China), allowing them to ferment without spoiling. Sprinkled with salt reddened with sacred alaea clay (a Hawaiian tradition), the salt-glazed poached eggs perch on top, looking like plump orbs in a nest, but when forked they release their fluid yolks over all.

Tear the leaves from the stems of the greens. Discard the stems and tear or cut the leaves into bite-size pieces. Heat the olive oil in a large skillet over medium-high heat. Add the garlic and pickled chiles, cooking until aromatic, about 30 seconds. Add the greens a few handfuls at a time, stirring as you do. Cover and cook until tender, about 5 minutes. Transfer to a bowl; keep warm.

Wipe out the skillet, fill with water, and bring to a boil. While the water is heating, crack 2 eggs into each of 4 coffee cups. Decrease the heat under the skillet so that the water barely simmers. Stir the sel gris into the water until the salt dissolves. Carefully slide the eggs from the cups into the simmering water. Simmer until the whites are fully set, 3 to 4 minutes. Spoon some water over the tops of the eggs to help set the surface of the yolks.

Lift the eggs from the poaching liquid with a slotted spatula. Arrange 2 eggs per person on a bed of the greens and peppers. Sprinkle some Molokai Red Sea Salt and pepper on the eggs. Serve immediately.

Continued

2 large bunches greens (such as collard, kale, mustard, or chard)

1 tablespoon olive oil

2 cloves garlic, minced

½ cup pickled chiles, chopped, jarred or homemade (page 86)

8 large or extra-large eggs, as fresh as possible

1 tablespoon briny sel gris (such as de Noirmoutier)

4 pinches Molokai Red Sea Salt

4 grindings black pepper

> ## SALT BOX
>
> Try Haleakala Ruby Sea Salt, or go black with Icelandic Lava Salt, Kilauea Onyx Sea Salt, or Black Lava Salt; or go vanilla with Fleur de Sel Guérande, Ilocano Asin, Aguni No Shio, or any semifine salt from a far-flung land.

Salt-Cured Pickled Chiles

MAKES 1 QUART

1 pound fresh red chiles, stemmed and sliced

¼ cup fine traditional salt (such as Yellowstone Natural Salt, Cuor di Trapani Sea Salt, Trapani e Marsala Sea Salt, or Sel Marin de Noirmoutier)

¼ cup white vinegar

Toss the chiles with the salt and pack into a clean quart jar. Cover with a clean towel and set at room temperature for 48 hours, stirring every 12 hours or so. Stir in the vinegar, screw a lid on the jar, and refrigerater for 5 days, stirring the peppers every day, until the peppers are fragrant and tender. They can be kept, refrigerated, nearly indefinitely, or for several years at least.

Salt Block–Fried Eggs with Grilled Tomatoes and Pork Belly

MAKES 2 SERVINGS

Himalayan pink salt is not the most distinctive-tasting salt in the world, but it is the only salt around that you can cook on. Once the block is hot (about 400°F), you cook on it just as you would a frying pan. The only difference is that the salt block will season your food as it cooks, and the salt will dehydrate the surface of the pork belly and eggs, yielding a lacquer-thin crispy skin.

You can ask your butcher to slice the pork belly into thick, 2-ounce slices the way he would bacon. Or, chill the piece of pork belly in the freezer just until firm, about 40 minutes, and cut into slices with a sharp knife. Sprinkle the belly with the sugar on both sides.

Place the salt block on a gas burner or on an electric burner with a heat diffuser. Heat over medium-low heat for 15 minutes. Raise the heat under the block to medium. Place the pork strips on the salt. Cook slowly until the pork is browned and looks cooked through, about 5 minutes per side. Have some paper towels ready to blot up excess rendered fat that can drip into the burner and cause a flare-up. Don't rush the cooking or the lean parts will overcook before the fatty parts have rendered. With that said, even when done the pork strips will not be completely crisp.

Carefully crack 2 eggs on top of each pork belly slice. Try to guide the eggs with a small spatula so that they land right on the bacon. The eggs will start to set up as soon as they hit the hot stone. Use your spatula to keep the whites from running over the edge of the stone. The fresher your eggs are, the less the whites will run. Cook for 3 to 4 minutes, until the whites are set but the yolks are still runny. Lift each portion of belly and eggs onto a plate and keep warm.

Season the tomato slices with pepper and cook on the salt block just until warmed through, about 30 seconds per side. Put 2 tomato slices on each plate and serve immediately with the toasted baguette.

¼ pound pork belly, cut lengthwise into 2 thick slices

2 teaspoons light or dark brown sugar

1 (8 or 9-inch) square salt block, about 2 inches thick

4 large eggs, as fresh as possible

1 ripe tomato, stem end trimmed, cut into 4 thick slices

Freshly ground black pepper

6 slices French baguette, toasted

Soft Scrambled Eggs with Fleur de Sel

MAKES 4 SERVINGS

I know you think you don't need a recipe for scrambled eggs, but I beg you to consider this: Eggs are delicate creatures and must be approached with care. Cooking them is all about feel. Rush the process and they will stiffen, but take your time and pay close attention and they will relax into luscious, indulgent curded custard. You want to salt them lightly beforehand, with something fine, like fleur de sel, and then sprinkle the finished dish with contrasting nuggets of something crunchy.

8 large or extra-large eggs

⅓ cup milk or cream

2 pinches fleur de sel, plus more for serving

¼ teaspoon freshly ground pepper

1 tablespoon unsalted butter

2 ounces fresh goat cheese

SALT BOX

Look for a coarser fleur de sel, like Fleur de Sel de l'Île de Noirmoutier, Flor de Sal de Manzanillo, Fiore di Galia, Fiore di Trapani, Bitterman's Fleur de Sel, or for color, Black Lava Salt. Alternatively, try a coarser salt, like Sel Gris de l'Île de Ré, Dolce di Cervia, or for color and flavor, Haleakala Ruby Sea Salt.

Crack the eggs into a bowl. Beat with a large fork or whisk until well combined. Add the milk, salt, and pepper and continue beating until foamy.

Put a 10-inch nonstick frying pan over the lowest heat possible. Add the butter and heat just until the butter melts. Tilt the pan to coat the bottom evenly with butter.

Add the beaten eggs to the pan and wait until you can see a few soft curds forming along the bottom of the pan. This will take 2 to 3 minutes. Using a sturdy plastic spatula, gently scrape the egg from the bottom of the pan. Keep scraping slowly until a moist, soft custard forms. This will take about 15 minutes.

Crumble the goat cheese into the eggs and keep scraping and turning the soft mound of custardy egg until it is set to the degree of doneness you want. Immediately scrape onto a plate. Sprinkle with fleur de sel and serve with more fleur de sel at the table for anyone who wants to really live it up.

Ricotta Pancakes with Vanilla Salt

MAKES 4 SERVINGS

Flour-laden pancakes, regardless of the type of flour used, be it buckwheat, cornmeal, or plain old wheat, long for sweetening—real maple syrup, golden treacle, or the over-the-top maplessence of imitation maple corn syrup. But remove the flour, or replace it with something more savory, and you get a pancake that's open for improvisation. This one is a spin on the ricotta cheese filling for cannoli or blintzes, reinforced with enough egg to stand up on its own. The ethereal results are poof-in-your-mouth puff pillows punctuated by flakes of sea salt and vanilla specks. You and your guests will be able to eat a pile, so you might consider doubling the recipe. These pancakes are equally good made with cottage cheese, but whether you use ricotta or cottage cheese you need to get it as dry as possible before making the batter. Suspending the cheese in a strainer lined with dampened cheesecloth for about 20 minutes does the trick.

Toss the strawberries and 2 tablespoons of the sugar in a small bowl; set aside.

Mix the ricotta cheese, egg yolks, remaining 4 tablespoons of sugar, flour, vanilla, and a pinch of the vanilla salt in a bowl. Beat the egg whites to soft peaks in a clean bowl with a balloon whisk, or in a stand mixer with the whisk attachment, and fold into the ricotta mixture.

Heat a griddle or 2 large frying pans over medium-high heat. Coat the hot pan(s) with the butter. Make 2 to 3-inch pancakes on the hot griddle and brown on both sides, flipping after 2 to 3 minutes. You should get 12 pancakes. Serve with the strawberries, which by now should have released enough liquid to dissolve the sugar. Top with the remaining vanilla salt.

12 strawberries, sliced

6 tablespoons sugar, divided

2 cups drained ricotta cheese

6 large or extra-large eggs, separated

6 tablespoons all-purpose flour

½ teaspoon vanilla extract

3½ teaspoons Taha'a Vanilla, divided

2 tablespoons unsalted butter

SALT BOX

If you don't have ready-made vanilla salt, see DIY Vanilla Salt (page 78).

Salt-Studded Grilled Cheese Sandwich

MAKES 1 SANDWICH

Great grilled cheese, like great salt, is a revelation, not so much because either is that much better than other edible marvels (though they are), but because we take both for granted. When you eat anything thoughtlessly, thinking about it automatically produces awe. Great grilled cheese requires only butter, and a molten mass of melted cheese bedded down between slices of beautifully browned and crisped bread studded with hulking, crunchy, tangy salt crystals. But why stop there? This sandwich may be shameless, but at least you won't take it for granted.

2 tablespoons unsalted butter, softened

2 thick slices fluffy egg bread (such as challah or brioche loaf)

2 tablespoons mayonnaise

2 teaspoons gochujang

2 or 3 thin slices ripe tomato

1 small sour pickle, sliced lengthwise into 4 slices

1½ ounces sliced white cheddar cheese

1½ ounces sliced yellow cheddar cheese

½ to 1 teaspoon Black Lava Salt

Generously butter one side of each slice of the bread. Mix the mayonnaise and gochujang in a small bowl. Spread on the unbuttered sides of each bread slice. Top one slice with tomato, the other with pickle slices. Cover the tomato slices with the white cheddar and the pickle slices with the yellow cheddar.

Set a large skillet over the lowest heat possible. Put the cheese-topped bread slices in the skillet, butter side down. Cover the skillet and cook until the cheese has melted, about 10 minutes. Do not rush. Check every now and then to make sure the bread is not burning. If it is and you are on the lowest heat you possible can get, you will have to stop and serve the sandwiches at their present state of melt.

Scatter the salt over the melted cheese of one of the slices and flip one half over the other so the salt is imbedded between the two cheese layers. Transfer to a plate, carefully cut in half, and tuck in.

> SALT BOX
>
> **Black Diamond Flake Salt, Kilauea Onyx Sea Salt, Icelandic Lava Salt, or a red salt or sel gris of choice**

CHAPTER 5

VEGETABLES AND FRUIT

Some vegetables—lettuces, radishes, spring onions, and cucumbers—are best served raw. Zucchini, cabbages, spinach, kale, green beans, sweet corn, and cauliflower are fine raw but are enhanced by some heat. Others, such as broccoli, asparagus, eggplant, turnips, rutabaga, and beets, are definitely better off cooked. And just a few, like potatoes, yams, and winter squash, are too tough or starchy to eat without thorough cooking. But all vegetables, regardless of how you prepare them, benefit from salting.

In general, how you cook a vegetable determines how you salt it. If you're feeling overt, the wetness and crunch of raw vegetables go well with crisp flake salt, and if you want subtlety, try fleur de sel or shio. Blanched or lightly cooked vegetables should be salted twice—during cooking with sel gris or traditional salt, and with fleur de sel or flake for finishing. Fully cooked veggies can stand maximum salting with hearty crystals like sel gris. Try briny sel gris for both cooking and finishing, or add color with black or red salt at the finish. Potatoes are delicious with smoked salt.

Salts are minerals, and they react both physically and chemically with all food. When it comes to vegetables, you can:

1. Salt for taste: Vegetables and fruit are both low in sodium and therefore can take assertive salting, but adding salt during cooking does little to develop their flavor since their main flavorful elements, sugars and esters, don't react with salt the way meat proteins do. The general rule with vegetables is: Salt at the end to add a counterpoint to their natural sweet green and fruity flavors. As with any rule, there are exceptions, as with potatoes and beans, for example.

2. Salt for cooking: The texture and color of boiled or blanched vegetables can be improved with salt. Salting vegetable cooking water makes it alkaline because sodium ions from the

salt displace calcium ions in the hemicellulose that holds plant fibers together. This increases the speed at which vegetables soften during boiling. This same salt-induced alkalinity also neutralizes the slight acidity of green vegetables, keeping them greener during blanching.

3. Salt for fermentation: All vegetables harbor beneficial (probiotic) bacteria. By submerging vegetables in a large amount of salt (about 7 percent), you can encourage the growth of this beneficial bacteria and discourage harmful bacteria. The beneficial bacteria feed off sugars in the vegetables, causing them to ferment into pickles.

4. Salt eggplants: Eggplants soak up oil like sponges during cooking. To limit the absorption, eggplant slices can be salted beforehand, which collapses their spongy structure and pulls out some water before they hit the oil, resulting in a crisper, firmer fry.

SALTS			FRUITS					VEGETABLES					
			raw	roasted	grilled	fried	cured/pickled	raw	steamed	roasted	grilled	fried	cured/pickled
	fleur de sel		X	X	X	X	X	X	X	X	X	X	X
	sel gris		X	X			X			X	X		X
	flake	fine	X		X	X		X	X	X	X	X	
		coarse	X	X	X	X		X	X	X	X		
	traditional	fine	X			X	X	X	X	X	X	X	X
		coarse	X	X			X			X	X		X
	shio						X	X	X	X		X	X
	rock	fine			X	X				X			X
		coarse					X						X
		block	X				X	X			X		X
	infused	smoked		X	X	X				X	X	X	
		flavored		X	X	X				X	X	X	

Avocado Toast

MAKES 4 SERVINGS

The avocado is one of the only fruits that develop fat rather than sweetness as it ripens (olives are the only other). In the kitchen, avocados are closer to butter than they are to other produce. No wonder about the craze for spreading them on bread. You may already be adding no more than good salt and oil to your avocado and toast. We've embellished this simple sandwich with a tahini spread for added richness and a flock of cucumber ribbons for vegetal moisture and a crunch that resonates even more with some audaciously crunchy salt.

Mix the tahini with half of the lime zest, 1 teaspoon of the lime juice, a pinch of the red pepper flakes, half of the black pepper, and the smoked salt in a small bowl. Set aside.

Cut ribbons of cucumber by running a vegetable peeler down the length of the cucumber until you reach the core of seeds. Rotate the cucumber one-third turn and repeat the ribbon-making process. Repeat with the final third of the cucumber. Discard the seed core or use in a salad. Toss the cucumber ribbons with 1 teaspoon of the lime juice, the remaining black pepper, and the fleur de sel.

Spread some of the tahini mixture on the toasted bread slices. Put an avocado half on each and smash flat with a fork. Sprinkle with the remaining lime zest, lime juice, and red pepper flakes and drizzle with the olive oil. Fold a few cucumber ribbons on top of each toast. Sprinkle with the black salt and serve immediately.

¼ cup sesame tahini

Finely grated zest and juice of 1 lime, divided

2 pinches red pepper flakes, divided

4 grindings black pepper, divided

¼ teaspoon smoked salt

1 medium cucumber

Pinch of fleur de sel

4 thick slices sourdough bread, toasted

2 avocados, halved lengthwise, pitted, and peeled

1 teaspoon extra-virgin olive oil

2 big pinches Black Diamond Flake Salt

SALT BOX

Hakanai Flake Salt, arguably the best avocado salt in the world, is a great alternative to the visually dramatic Black Diamond Flake Salt. Hakanai's close companions at the uppermost echelons of flake salt perfection include Havsnø Flaksalt, Bitterman's Flake, Achill Island Sea Salt, Murray River Salt, Hana Flake Salt, and J.Q. Dickinson.

Tossed Red Salad with Shallot Vinaigrette and Flake Salt

MAKES 4 SERVINGS

Crispy, crunchy crystals of flake salt fulfill their culinary destiny on top of a salad. Assuming the role of nature's croutons, any flake salt will work. Cyprus Silver Flake and Halen Môn Silver Flake are more dramatic, but I love the more delicate flake salts like Bitterman's Flake, Murray River, Havsnø Flaksalt, and Hakanai Flake, which all have very fine, very delicate flakes. Beneath the salt, this salad is quite tame, which underscores the transformative power of strategic salting.

1 shallot, halved and thinly sliced

3 tablespoons flavorful wine vinegar (we use equal parts red wine, rice wine, and sherry)

1 teaspoon Dijon mustard

3 tablespoons extra-virgin olive oil

3 grindings black pepper

1 head red leaf lettuce, broken into leaves

1 head radicchio, broken into leaves

4 big pinches flake salt

Combine the shallot and vinegar in a small bowl. Set aside for at least 15 minutes or as long as several hours.

When you are ready to make the salad, whisk the mustard, olive oil, and pepper into the vinegar mixture. Break the lettuces into bite-size pieces and toss with the vinaigrette in a salad bowl. Divide among serving plates and sprinkle each salad with flake salt. Serve immediately.

Fermented Cucumber Pickles

MAKES 1 QUART

Think of salt as a traffic cop for pickling. When you ferment cucumbers into pickles, you put them in a solution of salt and water—a brine that is about 7 percent salt. That's twice as salty as ocean water. Only two kinds of bacteria (both of which are good) can thrive at that level of salinity: *Leuconostoc mesenteroides* and *Lactobacillus plantarum*. Both start to grow and crowd out all the other bacteria. All bacteria, both helpful and harmful, produce acids as they grow. At a certain point, the brine gets so sour that the *Leuconostoc* bacteria can't survive and the probiotic *Lactobacillus* take over to create these full-sour pickles aromatic with black and red peppers. Salt isn't simply adding flavor; it's directing how flavor gets developed.

Put the salt and 1 cup hot tap water in the measuring cup. Stir until dissolved and add 1 cup of cold tap water.

Put the cucumbers in a quart jar vertically so that they are standing on end. They should fit tightly, which will help to keep the cucumbers submerged once the brine is added. Fit the garlic cloves around the cucumbers. Sprinkle the black peppercorns and pepper flakes, if using, on top. Add enough of the saltwater brine to the jar to completely cover the contents, leaving about 1 inch of space at the top of the jar. If you have any brine left, save it. You might need it to top off the pickles as they ferment. Cover with a lid, but do not screw the lid on tightly.

Set in a cool room (about 65°F) away from direct sunlight for about 1 week to ferment. As the pickles ferment, bubbles of CO_2 gas will become visible inside the jar. Check the pickles daily to make sure no mold is forming. If the brine level should fall below the top of the pickles, top it off with more saltwater brine.

Start tasting after 4 days. When the pickles are to your liking, refrigerate them, which will slow down the fermentation. As they are stored, the pickles will continue to ferment and become more sour. Kept under refrigeration, they will not spoil.

3 tablespoons fleur de sel or fine traditional salt

1 pound (6 to 8) small firm cucumbers (not burpless)

4 cloves garlic, peeled, halved if large

½ teaspoon cracked black peppercorns

Pinch of red pepper flakes (optional)

SALT BOX

In a pickle, any fine craft salt will work. Note that salts sold as pickling salt are just salt with no added iodine, as iodine will discolor a pickle and also contribute a bitter, acrid flavor.

Grilled Endive Salad with Salted Garlic and Parmesan Crumble

MAKES 4 SERVINGS

This takeoff on a grilled Caesar salad replaces romaine with two colors of chicory lettuce—pale Belgian endive and scarlet radicchio. Both of these leaves are far more bitter than romaine, elevating the contrapuntal between vegetable, dressing, cheese, and salt.

⅓ cup freshly grated Parmigiano-Reggiano cheese

1 clove garlic, smashed and minced

6 anchovy fillets, minced

1 tablespoon brown mustard

1 large egg yolk

½ cup plus 2 tablespoons extra-virgin olive oil, divided

Juice of 1 lemon

Sea salt and freshly ground black pepper

Mild vegetable oil, for coating grill grate

4 heads Belgian endive, halved lengthwise

1 head radicchio, loose leaves removed, quartered through its stem

1 teaspoon coarse flake sea salt

Preheat the oven to 400°F. Line a sheet pan with a silicone baking liner or parchment paper.

Make 4 mounds of cheese on the lined pan, evenly spaced. They will each be a heaping tablespoon. Lightly pat each mound so that it is flat on top. Bake until brown and crisp, 8 to 10 minutes. Cool.

Preheat a grill to medium indirect heat (300° to 350°F).

Mash the garlic and anchovy into a paste in a small bowl using the back of a fork. Whisk in the mustard and egg yolk. Whisk in ½ cup of the olive oil, a little at a time, to form a thick sauce. Stir in the lemon juice and season with salt and pepper; set aside.

Brush the grill grate and coat with vegetable oil. Coat the pieces of endive and radicchio with the remaining 2 tablespoons of olive oil. Put the endive on the grill grate directly over the fire. Grill for about 1 minute; turn. Add the radicchio and grill for another minute, turning the radicchio after 30 seconds, just until grill marked. Using tongs, transfer the pieces of both lettuces to the cool side of the grill. Paint with half the vinaigrette, getting dressing down in between the leaves. Cover the grill and cook for 2 minutes, until the ends of the endive halves wilt.

Put the endives and radicchio on a platter. Dress with the remaining vinaigrette. Crumble the cheese crisps over the top and finish with a sprinkling of flake salt.

SALT BOX

Halen Môn Silver Flake Sea Salt,
Cyprus Silver Flake Sea Salt,
Maldon Sea Salt, Cornish Flake
Sea Salt, Hana Flake Salt

Black Truffle Salt Smashed Potatoes

MAKES 4 SERVINGS

A potato is a potato when it comes to salting. Each and every one needs it. But truffle salt is something every potato *wants*. They yearn for it, pine for it, sing the blues for it, post pictures on Instagram of it. They are all so needy—so how do we choose which potato will be graced with our hard-earned truffle salt? Depends. Just as we salt-loving humans might divide ourselves into categories (window or aisle, single stuff or double stuff), potatoes likewise fall into two culinary categories: Mealy potatoes (russets, baking potatoes, blues) yield a soft, floury consistency and very little cohesive structure, making them great for baking, roasting, and mashing; and waxy potatoes (red round, all-purpose whites), which hold their shape as they soften, making them gummy when mashed, but creamy on the inside and crispy on the outside when smashed. Here, we want the creamy-on-the-inside crusty-on-the-outside heaven that is a smashed potato.

8 medium-small round red or yellow potatoes

2 teaspoons olive oil

1 teaspoon Black Truffle Salt, plus more for garnish

¼ cup vegetable oil

SALT BOX

Use Black Truffle Salt on scrambled eggs, macaroni and cheese, wild mushroom risotto, potato and vegetable gratin, potato chips, grilled asparagus, deviled eggs, popcorn, and mashed into unsalted butter to make truffle butter that can go on anything from steaks to string beans.

Preheat the oven to 400°F.

Rub the potatoes with the olive oil, put on a sheet pan, and roast until tender, about 40 minutes. Remove from the oven and keep on the pan; cool for at least 20 minutes, or as long as several hours.

Make a cross cut in the top of each potato, push open a bit, and sprinkle each with a pinch of truffle salt. Smash each potato with a flat meat pounder, small heavy skillet, or large rubber mallet into a flattened ¾-inch-thick disk. One good thwack should do it. Pick up any bits of potato flesh that have gone flying and reintegrate into their source.

Heat the vegetable oil in a medium skillet over medium-high heat. Add the potatoes to the hot oil (4 at a time is usually what will fit comfortably) and cook until brown and crisp on both sides. Flip after about 2 minutes.

Serve slit side up, scattered with more truffle salt.

French Fries 2.0

Potatoes are glorified by deep frying. This is no secret and has been well known since the 19th century, when they were all the rage in Britain, where richness in cooking was attributed to the French (hence the name, french fry), while in France they are simply called fried potatoes, or *pommes frites*. French fries provide the true frites freak with a golden-brown playground for some spectacular salting. My four favorite tricks to take fries to the next level:

- Using russet potatoes, which are high in starch content, yields the flakiest fries that stay crisp longer than fries made from waxy potatoes.
- Soaking cut potatoes in water prior to frying draws starch to the surface of the potato, creating a greater potential for a thick, crisp crust.
- Double-frying your frites creates flavor and crunch that great restaurants might rival but will never surpass.
- I go with finely ground rock salt, which clings lovingly to the fry and then strikes from out of nowhere to deliver its tangy bite.

In a large bowl, stir 1 tablespoon of the salt into the ice water. Add the potatoes and let soak for 10 minutes.

In a large, heavy deep saucepan or electric deep fryer, heat 4 to 5 inches of oil over medium heat to 325°F.

Drain the potatoes and dry thoroughly with paper towels. Fry the potatoes, in batches, until tender and lightly browned at the tips, about 6 minutes per batch. Using a slotted spoon, remove the potatoes from the oil and drain on paper towels. Repeat with the remaining potatoes, adjusting the heat as necessary between batches. Let stand at room temperature for up to 2 hours.

Return the oil to medium heat and heat to 375°F. Fry the potatoes again in small batches until golden brown and crisp, about 3 minutes per batch. Using a slotted spoon, remove the potatoes from the oil and drain on paper towels. Season to taste with some of the remaining salt and serve immediately. Repeat with the remaining potatoes, adjusting the heat as necessary between batches.

2 tablespoons fine Himalayan Pink Salt, divided

4 cups ice water

2 pounds russet potatoes, cut into ¾-inch-thick rods

Vegetable oil, for frying

SALT BOX

Finely ground Himalayan Pink Salt, Persian Blue Salt, Redmond Real Salt, Yellowstone Natural Salt, Vancouver Island Sea Salt, Saltwest Naturals Sea Salt, Sel Marin de Noirmoutier

Charred Padrón Peppers with Brazilian Sal Grosso

MAKES 4 APPETIZER SERVINGS

My first encounter of this dish was in a small fishing town in Galicia, Spain, where these peppers just happen to come from. Padrón peppers are small and generally vivid green, although you may be lucky enough to find a ripe red one. Most are quite tame, but on occasion you happen across one that's vividly hot. It's impossible to tell a hot padrón from a mild one by looks alone, which is part of the fun. But sitting at a tiny metal table on a small cobbled street in the early evening warmth, drinking ice-cold beer, the spicy ones were not what caught my attention. It was the salt: coarse, silvery, copious, rained down with reckless abandon. Every bite was a freefall of sensory bliss, and only once in a while did a hot pepper remind me that it might not last forever. If you cannot find padróns, shishito peppers will work, though they lack the intermittent fire.

¼ cup olive oil

2 cloves garlic, thinly sliced

8 ounces padrón peppers

1 tablespoon Brazilian Sal Grosso

12 hazelnuts, chopped

½ lemon

Heat the olive oil in a large cast-iron skillet over high heat until it shimmers, about 2 minutes. It should be about ¼ inch deep.

Add the garlic and peppers in a single layer. They shouldn't crowd the pan. Sauté until the peppers are charred in spots, turning with tongs every now and then. It will take about 3 minutes. Scatter the salt and hazelnuts on top and sauté for another minute. Drain on paper towels and serve squirted with lemon juice.

> ## SALT BOX
>
> **Coarse, hard salt is what you need: Sal de Ibiza Granito, Dolce di Cervia, Piran Sel Gris, Redmond Real Salt, Himalayan Pink Salt, or Persian Blue Salt.**

Curried Roasted Peaches
with Honey and Kala Namak

MAKES 4 SERVINGS

Kala Namak is traditionally made by combining ordinary salt, like pink salt from Pakistan, with charcoal, spices, and other botanicals until it melts. It is then cooled, aged, and ground. When finished, the salt is rich in iron sulfide, which contributes to its red-black color and gives it the aroma of hard-cooked eggs. Attributed with multiple health properties, it is also magical in cooking, bringing heartiness to popcorn, meatiness to curried vegetables, and powers of levitation to roasted peaches.

4 large barely ripe peaches

⅔ cup bourbon

3 tablespoons honey

1 teaspoon vanilla extract

2 tablespoons unsalted butter, melted

2 teaspoons garam masala

½ teaspoon ground turmeric

¼ teaspoon saffron threads, crumbled

½ teaspoon finely ground Kala Namak

Preheat the oven to 425°F.

Halve the peaches and remove the pits. Fit the peaches, cut side up, snugly in a baking dish. Mix the bourbon, honey, vanilla, butter, garam masala, and turmeric in a small bowl; spoon over the peaches. Roast until soft and slightly wrinkled, about 35 minutes, basting with pan juices every 15 minutes.

Mix the saffron and Kala Namak. Sprinkle each peach with a pinch of this mixture. Cool for 5 minutes, to allow the salt to dissolve and the color of the saffron to bloom. Serve warm.

NAMAK BOX

Kala Namak can be used in chaats, chutneys, raitas, fruit salads, savory or bready fried snacks, soups, tofu, and in all manner of South Asian cuisines from Bangledeshi to Pakistani.

Block-Salted Watermelon
with Green Peppercorns and Black Salt

MAKES 4 SERVINGS

We think that watermelon is loaded with sugar, when in fact it is lower in carbohydrates than any other melon. The reason it tastes so monolithically sweet is because it is significantly low in sodium. A glaze of salt from a brief sojourn on a chilled salt block helps make the taste of sliced watermelon whole.

Put the salt block in the freezer for 1 hour or longer.

Arrange the watermelon slices in a single layer on the chilled block. Set aside for 5 minutes; turn over and let rest for 3 more minutes. At this point, remove the watermelon from the block. It is best to proceed right away, but you can refrigerate the watermelon slices for up to 4 hours, if necessary.

Shingle the slices on a serving platter and sprinkle both types of peppercorns and the black salt over the top. Serve immediately.

1 (8 or 9-inch) square salt block of any thickness

4 (1-inch-thick) semicircular slices halved watermelon, rind removed

2 teaspoons dried green peppercorns, cracked

½ teaspoon black peppercorns, cracked

1 teaspoon crunchy black salt

SALT BOX

Icelandic Lava Salt, Black Diamond Flake Salt, Kilauea Onyx Sea Salt, Black Lava Salt, or a hearty fleur de sel such as Sugpo Asin or Flor de Sal do Algarve, Bitterman's Fleur de Sel

Saffron-Salted Roasted Cauliflower and Tomatoes

MAKES 4 SERVINGS

Vegetables are full of flavor, but they are also full of water. Getting rid of the water concentrates the flavor, but it also alters their consistency. With sturdy cauliflower and squishable tomatoes, those consistency changes are profound, but they require different roasting techniques to get the desired results. Low heat is helpful when roasting tomatoes, which at high temperatures collapse into purée. On the other hand, cauliflower becomes delectably creamy when roasted at high heat. So by roasting tomatoes slowly and cauliflower quickly, you end up with a perfect pair. Now all that's needed is a gilding of Saffron Salt, and voilà!

Preheat the oven to 200°F.

Toss the tomatoes, garlic, 4 teaspoons of the olive oil, fleur de sel, and pepper on a rimmed sheet pan. Shake the pan to make everything slide into a single layer.

Roast until the tomatoes have shrunk by about 50 percent and no longer appear wet on their surface, about 4 hours. No need to peek or toss during cooking, and there is no harm if they roast for an extra hour.

Cool for 15 minutes to help them firm up, and then scrape off the pan using a rubber spatula or wooden spoon.

While the tomatoes are cooling turn the oven temperature up to 425°F.

Toss the cauliflower florets and onion wedges with the remaining 2 teaspoons of oil on the sheet pan. Spread them out in a single layer and sprinkle with 1 teaspoon saffron salt. Roast for 15 minutes.

Check the cauliflower, as it should be browning. Add the roasted tomatoes and toss to disperse the tomatoes evenly and to turn the cauliflower and onions. Roast for 10 more minutes, or until the cauliflower is fork-tender.

Sprinkle with the remaining 1 teaspoon of saffron salt and serve.

1 pound plum tomatoes, quartered lengthwise

2 cloves garlic, finely chopped

2 tablespoons extra-virgin olive oil, divided

1 teaspoon fleur de sel

1 teaspoon coarsely ground black pepper

1 head cauliflower, cut into bite-size florets

1 medium yellow onion, cut into thin wedges through the stem end so wedges stay intact

2 teaspoons Saffron Salt, divided

SALT BOX

Pesto Flake Salt, Rosemary Flake Salt, Sage Salt, or go classic minimalist and just use a fleur de sel.

CHAPTER 6

GRAINS

You name the grain, salt is what transforms mere carbohydrates into the staff of life. Left whole, with the germ and bran intact, grains deliver a subtle range of nutty, savory, and bittersweet flavors. After processing, when nothing but the bulky, starchy endosperm is left, grains and the products made from them become veritable flavor vacuums, demanding a hefty dose of salt just to make them palatable.

But often salting does much more than just shape and amplify flavor. Salt plays a structural role in the formation of dough, particularly bread dough, enhancing chewiness and ensuring proper rising. At 1.5 to 2 percent of the flour's weight, salt helps to tighten gluten and increase the finished bread's volume. The presence of magnesium and calcium in most unrefined craft salts increases their ability to strengthen gluten over that of refined table or kosher salt. On the other hand, the levels of salt needed to help gluten can inhibit the growth of yeasts. Salt is added to sourdoughs early on to limit the activity of souring bacteria that can damage gluten formation. With other yeasted doughs, salt is usually added after the yeast is given some time to reproduce.

There are fewer technical considerations when salting other grains, such as pasta and rice. It is difficult to oversalt such starchy grain dishes, making them prime candidates for layering the varying flavors, colors, and textures that come from salting at multiple times in the preparation—also an invitation to use several types of craft salt in a single dish.

GRAINS

			bread	flatbread	pretzels	whole grains	salads	risotto	noodles	popcorn
S A L T S	fleur de sel		X	X	X	X	X	X	X	X
	sel gris				X			X	X	
	flake	fine	X	X	X	X	X	X		X
		coarse			X		X	X	X	
	traditional	fine	X	X		X	X			X
		coarse							X	
	shio					X	X	X		X
	rock	fine	X	X	X					X
		coarse			X					
		block		X	X					
	infused	smoked	X	X	X	X	X	X	X	X
		flavored	X	X	X	X	X	X	X	X

Truffled Wild Mushroom Risotto

Black Truffle Salt is the most cost-effective way to bring truffles into your diet. A whole jar will cost you about the same as one or two shavings of good truffle, and it lasts much longer, so you can amortize the purchase over many meals. In this dish, dried wild mushrooms and a flock of fresh cremini augment the flavor of truffle. Cremini possess a meaty texture that is just the thing to back up the pungent compost aroma of truffle. Aside from all the fungi, this is a straightforward risotto recipe. You will notice the wild mushrooms are added at the start and the truffle salt at the finish. That's to build up the rice with a sylvan umami foundation capable of supporting momentous truffle aroma.

Soak the porcini mushrooms in the boiling water in a bowl until softened, about 10 minutes. Drain (retaining the soaking liquid), and coarsely chop the mushrooms.

Heat the oil in a large saucepan over medium-high heat. Add the onion and sauté until tender, about 3 minutes. Add the cremini mushrooms, garlic, and rosemary, and sauté until they lose their raw look.

Add the rice and sauté until coated with oil. Add the vermouth and bring to a boil, stirring often. Boil until the mixture no longer smells of alcohol. Decrease the heat so that the liquid simmers. Stir in the reserved mushroom soaking liquid and continue stirring until it has almost all been absorbed. Stir in the soaked mushrooms and the broth in 3 additions, 1 cup at a time, waiting until the last addition is almost completely absorbed before adding the next.

When the last addition has been absorbed about halfway, taste the rice. It should be tender but still chewy in the center. Add the truffle salt, butter, and both cheeses. Simmer until a rich, flowing sauce forms, about 2 minutes. Serve immediately.

1 ounce dried porcini mushrooms or other dried wild mushrooms

1½ cups boiling water

2 tablespoons olive oil

1 medium yellow onion, finely chopped

1 pound cremini or foraged mushrooms, sliced, halved before slicing if large

3 cloves garlic, minced

1 teaspoon dried rosemary

1 cup Arborio or Carnaroli rice

1 cup dry vermouth

3 cups broth (mushroom, vegetable, or chicken)

2 teaspoons truffle salt

2 tablespoons unsalted butter

1 cup freshly grated Parmigiano-Reggiano cheese

1 cup mascarpone cheese

Seven-Salt Focaccia

MAKES 12 SERVINGS

Focaccia and pizza are similar, but not interchangeable. They're both southern Italian flatbreads topped with colorful flavorful ingredients, but pizza is more about the topping, and salt often comes in the form of cheese (salted milk curds), sauce (from the Latin *salsus*, meaning "salted"), or salami (from the vulgar Latin *salamen*, "to salt"). Focaccia is more about the bread, and salting trends toward elemental, crystalline sea salt. Focaccia dough usually includes an ingredient that relaxes its chewiness. Ours has a considerable amount of extra-virgin olive oil, but others, like the dense, herb-infused focaccia of Puglia (the heel of the boot), include cooked potato as a tenderizer. Pizzas are typically topped with sauce and cheese, but focaccia topping is simpler—a few chopped herbs, slices of sun-dried tomato, a dusting of dry cheese, and always a considerable crust of salt. This focaccia is topped with seven salts. Although you can use any combination you want, we suggest a variety of colors, textures, and flavors.

5¼ cups bread flour, divided

2 teaspoons plus pinch of active dry yeast, divided

2 cups warm water (110° to 115°F), divided

¾ cup extra-virgin olive oil, divided

5 teaspoons fleur de sel

1 teaspoon each: rock salt, flake salt, red salt, black salt, smoked salt, Pesto Flake Salt, and truffle salt

Mix 1¾ cups of the flour, a pinch of yeast, and 1 cup of the warm water in a bowl until combined. Cover loosely with plastic wrap, and let rise at room temperature for 8 to 12 hours, until almost tripled in volume.

Combine the remaining 3½ cups flour, remaining 2 teaspoons of yeast, remaining 1 cup of warm water, ½ cup of the oil, and the risen mixture in the bowl of a stand mixer fitted with a dough hook. Mix on low speed to moisten the dry ingredients, about 4 minutes, scraping the sides of the bowl as needed with a rubber spatula. Increase the mixer speed to medium and mix until the dough is smooth and clings to the dough hook, about 8 minutes. Add the fleur de sel to the bowl and mix on medium speed until the dough is very smooth, about 4 minutes.

Put the dough in an oiled bowl, turning it to coat with oil, cover with plastic wrap, and set in a warm place until doubled in size, about 1 hour.

Using a bowl scraper or a large mixing spoon dipped in flour, scrape the dough onto a heavily floured surface. Pat the dough with floured hands into a ½-inch-thick rectangle, and fold it into thirds as you would a letter.

Coat a rimmed half sheet pan with the remaining ¼ cup of oil. Press the dough out into the pan, turning it to coat both sides with oil. Continue to press and stretch the dough to fit the pan. As you do this, spread your fingers out, making finger holes through the dough to create a craggy surface that allows more salt to cling to the top. If you don't puncture holes all the way through the dough, the finished bread, after rising, will be too smooth.

Cover with a clean kitchen towel. Put in a warm place and let rise until air bubbles form under the surface of the dough and the dough is light and airy, about doubled in size, about 1 hour more.

Preheat the oven to 450°F.

Mix the 7 salts together and sprinkle over the top of the bread, pressing lightly into the surface. Bake for 20 minutes, or until the bread is golden and crusty. Decrease the oven temperature to 400°F and bake until dark brown, about 10 more minutes. Remove and let cool on a cooling rack.

SALT BOX

What better way to celebrate focaccia than with seven salts from Italy? Alas, it isn't so easy to do. In the old days, you could count on Italy to provide you with dozens, even hundreds, of different craft salts. Most all traditional saltworks are now gone, but a few do remain. If we allow ourselves to travel just a little beyond Italy's modern borders to Slovenia (which used to be part of the Venetian empire), we can get there: Black Truffle Salt, Fiore di Galia, Fiore di Trapani, Fiore di Cervia, Dolce di Cervia, Piran Sel Gris, coarsely ground Trapani e Marsala Sea Salt.

Smoked Salt Soft Pretzels

MAKES 6 SERVINGS

Part of my childhood was spent in New York City, and the guy with the soft pretzel stand at the corner of Perry and Hudson was my surrogate father. Or so I sometimes wished. It's a crying shame that the firm, chewy, salt-crusted soft pretzels I loved so much as a child have turned into margarine-soaked fluff cakes hawked in every food court and airport. This recipe is dedicated to my adoptive pretzel family. I've respectfully modernized them with smoked salt, but you can always go old school with an unsmoked coarse traditional or rock salt.

1 cup warm water (110° to 115°F)

2 teaspoons active dry yeast

1 teaspoon sugar

¼ cup extra-virgin olive oil, divided

2 teaspoons sel gris, finely ground in a mortar and pestle or salt mill

2¾ cups bread flour, plus more if needed

¼ cup cornmeal

3 tablespoons baking soda

1 to 2 tablespoons coarse Maine Hickory Smoked Sea Salt

To prepare the pretzel dough, combine the water, yeast, and sugar in a large bowl, stirring until mixed. Let sit until foamy, about 5 minutes. Stir in 3 tablespoons of the olive oil, the sel gris, and flour, and stir into a kneadable dough.

Turn onto a floured surface and knead until the dough is smooth and elastic, about 5 minutes, adding more flour as needed to keep the dough from sticking to your hands or the work surface. Try to add as little additional flour as possible.

Coat a large bowl with the remaining 1 tablespoon of oil and add the dough, turning to coat it with the oil. Cover and let rise in a warm spot until doubled in bulk, about 1 hour, or overnight in the refrigerator.

Preheat the oven to 425°F. Sprinkle the cornmeal over the bottom of a large rimmed sheet pan.

Divide the dough into 6 equal pieces. Flour your hands and a work surface lightly with flour. Roll and stretch each piece into a rope about 18 inches long.

To form a pretzel:

1. Take an end of the dough rope in each hand. Bring one end of the rope in a loop across the center.
2. Bring the other side of the rope across the first side. Your hands and the dough rope will be crossed.
3. To form the knot in the center of the pretzel, uncross your hands and grab the end of the rope closest to each hand. Cross your hands again, bringing the end of the rope on the bottom over the top.
4. You should have something that resembles a pretzel. Push or pull as necessary to even it out and press down the ends so they stay in place.

Bring a quart of water to a boil in a large skillet. Stir in the baking soda, and adjust the heat so the water barely simmers. Carefully set the pretzels, one at a time, in the water and simmer until they puff, about 20 seconds per side. Lift them out with a slotted spatula or spoon, allowing the excess water to drip back into the skillet before putting them on the cornmeal-coated sheet pan. Sprinkle the tops of the pretzels with the smoked salt, and bake until golden brown, 12 to 15 minutes. Transfer to a cooling rack and cool for at least 20 minutes, to allow the pretzels to firm up and get a little chewy.

SALT BOX

Coarse smoked salts like Gulf Coast Pecan Smoked Salt, Sugar Maple Smoked Sea Salt, or au naturel with coarse Yellowstone Natural Salt, Piran Sel Gris, Dolce di Cervia, J.Q. Dickinson, or Popohaku Opal Sea Salt (my preferences in that order)

Arugula Pizza with Blue Cheese, Prosciutto, and Crispy Salt

MAKES 4 TO 6 SERVINGS

Throughout northern Italy, you will find stupendous thin-crust pizza with roasted or fresh greens and, if desired, a few slices of prosciutto. If you are like me and have received military-grade conditioning to never say no to prosciutto, it's a pizza that can tend to dominate your eating when traveling there. My usual response when someone asks me the impossible question, "What's your favorite salt?" is "prosciutto." The 20th century has wiped out most of Italy's salt heritage, so this recipe bridges the gap with salts from foreign shores. We make up for the intrusion with the inclusion of a bounty of quintessentially Italian flavors. The dough is baked with garlic, herbs, blue cheese, and sweet shallot vinaigrette. Then as soon as it comes from the oven, while still piping hot, a simple salad is mounded on top of the steaming crust, along with curls of paper-thin prosciutto and monumental crunches of flake salt.

PIZZA DOUGH

1 cup warm water (110° to 115°F)

2 teaspoons active dry yeast

1 teaspoon sugar

¼ cup extra-virgin olive oil, divided

2 teaspoons fleur de sel

2¾ cups bread flour, plus more if needed

PIZZA TOPPING

3 tablespoons extra-virgin olive oil, divided

½ cup shallot vinaigrette (see page 96), divided

1 clove garlic, minced

1 teaspoon fresh oregano or thyme leaves

8 ounces blue cheese, crumbled

1 large bunch baby arugula (about 6 ounces), stems removed (about 3 cups leaves)

2 ounces thinly sliced prosciutto (about 8 slices)

1 tablespoon coarse flake salt

Freshly ground black pepper

Continued

To prepare the dough, combine the water, yeast, and sugar in a large bowl, stirring until mixed. Let sit until foamy, about 5 minutes. Stir in 3 tablespoons of the olive oil, the fleur de sel, and flour, and stir into a kneadable dough.

Turn onto a floured surface and knead until the dough is smooth and elastic, about 5 minutes, adding more flour as needed to keep the dough from sticking to your hands or the work surface. Try to add as little additional flour as possible.

Coat a large bowl with the remaining 1 tablespoon of oil and add the dough, turning to coat it with the oil. Cover and let rise in a warm spot until doubled in bulk, about 1 hour, or overnight in the refrigerator.

Preheat the oven to 425°F. If you have a baking stone, place it in the oven to warm up. If you don't, line the middle rack with heavy-duty aluminum foil.

Oil a sheet pan with 1 tablespoon of oil. Press and stretch the dough on the sheet into a circle or oval ⅛ to ¼ inch thick. Don't bother making a rim around the edge of the crust unless you like it for aesthetics. Coat the top of the dough round with the remaining 2 tablespoons of oil.

Mix the vinaigrette, garlic, and oregano in a small bowl. Scatter the cheese over the dough. Drizzle with a couple of spoonfuls of the vinaigrette. Slide the pizza onto the hot stone or foil-lined oven rack and bake until the edges are puffed and browned and the cheese has melted, about 6 minutes.

SALT BOX

Bulls Bay Carolina Flake, Halen Môn Silver Flake Sea Salt, Cyprus Silver Flake Sea Salt, Maldon Sea Salt, Alaska Pure Sea Salt, Achill Island Sea Salt, Hana Flake Salt

When the pizza is ready, use a pizza peel or two large spatulas to slide it from the oven onto a cutting board. Toss the arugula with 3 tablespoons of the vinaigrette and brush the remaining vinaigrette over the pizza. Mound the arugula on top, covering the cheese. Nestle curled slices of prosciutto in the arugula, and scatter the whole thing liberally with flake salt and black pepper to taste. Cut into pieces and serve.

Fleur de Sel Fettuccine with Garlic and Cheese

MAKES 6 TO 8 SERVINGS

Pasta craves salt. It's one of the few dishes where you simply cannot skimp. Usually pasta's salt appetite is satiated by liberally salting the cooking liquid. That's fine. But what if you're having a really great day, fresh air, unexpected smiles? What if you want an irrepressible expression of life's goodness, the fullness and intensity of it all? Salting pasta water just may not seem like enough. In this dish, the noodles are affirmed with fleur de sel thrown right into the dough. If you want a dish that illustrates "Salarius Maximus" (see page 14), here you are. The silken noodles set the stage, but this pasta dish is all about salt, radiant, in love with extra-virgin oil, a whiff of garlic, and a liberal frisk of Parmigiano.

Mix the all-purpose and semolina flours and 1 tablespoon of the fleur de sel in the bowl of a stand mixer fitted with the paddle attachment. Add the eggs and oil, and mix just until the dough comes together, about 2 minutes.

Scrape the dough onto a lightly floured board and knead until the dough is smooth and elastic, about 5 minutes, using just enough additional flour to keep the dough from sticking to the work surface or your hands. The dough is ready when you stretch it between your hands and it pulls back readily. Mix the remaining 1 tablespoon of fleur de sel with 2 tablespoons flour and knead into the dough just until it is evenly dispersed.

Form the dough into a ball and flatten it into a disk. Cover and set aside to rest for 30 minutes, or wrap in plastic wrap and refrigerate for up to 3 days.

Continued

PASTA

1⅓ cups all-purpose flour, plus more for kneading

½ cup semolina flour

2 tablespoons fleur de sel of choice, divided

4 large eggs

1 tablespoon extra-virgin olive oil

Handful of Dolce di Cervia

SAUCE

¼ cup extra-virgin olive oil

6 cloves garlic, finely chopped

2 tablespoons unsalted butter

½ cup freshly grated Parmigiano-Reggiano cheese

½ teaspoon freshly ground black pepper

⅓ cup finely chopped fresh flat-leaf parsley

SALT BOX

This is such an unusual recipe that it defies the standard rules of salting. Fleur de sel is a natural way to go because the whole family of salt in general has such a delicious balance of minerals, and because it is fine enough to work in this application—unlike sel gris. Any medium-fine salt will work, but be sure your choice does have some texture to it; very fine salts dissolve too fast and will not give you some of the novel textural dimensions of this pasta.

Meanwhile, cut the dough into 4 equal pieces. If you refrigerated the dough, let the pieces sit at room temperature for 10 minutes to relax. Form each piece into a rectangle just wide enough to fit between the rollers of your pasta machine. Flour your work surface and set your pasta roller to its widest setting. Dust one of the dough pieces with flour and pass it through the rollers. Dust it with more flour and pass it through the widest setting again. Fold the dough sheet in half and cut off ¼ inch of the corners of the dough at the fold; this will help keep the dough sheet uniform. Narrow the rollers by one setting and pass the dough sheet through another one or two times. Fold the dough, snip the corners, and pass through the next narrower setting. Keep going until you have a sheet of pasta that is about as thick as a bed sheet. Flour the sheet as needed to keep it from sticking. You should end up with a sheet of pasta that is about 3 feet long and 6 inches wide. Repeat with the remaining sheets. If you don't have a pasta machine, the dough pieces can be rolled with a rolling pin on a floured board, but it is difficult to get the dough as thin and even rolling it by hand.

To cut the dough into noodles, lay a sheet of dough out flat on a lightly floured work surface. Cut it in half with a knife or cutting wheel and feed it through the fettuccine cutting blade of your pasta machine, cut edge first. Lay the cut noodles on a flat-weave towel while you cut the rest.

Bring a large pot of water to a boil and throw a handful of Dolce di Cervia into the boiling water. Put a large colander into a large bowl. Set in the sink. Add the pasta to the boiling water and stir to make sure all of the noodles are separate. Boil just long enough for the noodles to swell and cook through, about 2 minutes, stirring occasionally.

While the pasta is cooking, put the oil and garlic in a large deep skillet. Scoop 2 cups of water from the boiling pasta pot and add to the skillet. Bring to a boil.

Pour the pasta into the colander, capturing most of the water in the bowl and all of the pasta in the colander. Lift the pasta from the water, shaking out any excess, and add to the skillet. Crank the heat up under the skillet. Add the butter and toss together to get the noodles evenly coated. Add ¼ cup of the cheese, the pepper, and 1 more cup of the pasta water. Toss until a fluid sauce forms and the noodles are coated. Add the remaining ¼ cup of cheese and more pasta water, to make even more sauce. The noodles should be luxuriously coated with a creamy sauce. Toss in the parsley and serve immediately.

Three-Salt Ramen

MAKES 4 SERVINGS

If your notion of ramen is confined to cellophane packages and a hot plate in a dorm room, wake up and smell the shoyu. You can buy authentic fresh ramen noodles in many Asian markets, and dried ones everywhere. If all you've got is the cellophane packs, that's fine too; just throw out the flavor packet. In this recipe, three of the garnishes are premade for you—red salt, black salt, and some sort of killer shio.

6 cups pork or chicken broth

2 inches fresh ginger, thinly sliced

1 clove garlic, thinly sliced

2 tablespoons shoyu soy sauce

4 scallions, both white and green parts, very thinly sliced

¼ cup mirin

¼ cup white or red miso

½ teaspoon freshly ground white pepper

½ teaspoon toasted sesame oil

4 servings ramen noodles (8 ounces dry, 12 ounces fresh, or homemade page 124)

4 large eggs, hard-cooked and halved, or poached

1 cup bean sprouts

2 sheets toasted nori, each torn into 4 pieces (8 pieces total)

2 tablespoons sesame seeds, toasted

1 tablespoon red chili blend (such as Japanese shichimi togarashi)

1 teaspoon red salt

1 teaspoon black flake salt

1 teaspoon shio

Combine the broth, ginger, garlic, soy sauce, and half of the scallions in a soup pot. Bring to a boil, and simmer for 15 minutes. Strain and return the broth to the pot.

Add the mirin, miso, white pepper, and sesame oil. Simmer, whisking, until the broth is opaque, completely smooth (no lumps of miso), and slightly reduced, 8 to 10 minutes. Taste the broth for flavor—it should be very robust. Cover the broth and lower the heat to keep it warm until you're ready to serve.

When you're ready to serve, cook the ramen noodles in boiling water according to the package instructions. Drain them and transfer to warmed deep soup bowls. If the broth has cooled off, bring it to a simmer again. Ladle the hot broth into the bowls and then arrange an egg and some bean sprouts on top. Place a couple of toasted nori sheets on the side of the bowl or in the bowl and sprinkle on the sesame seeds, the remaining scallions, and chili flakes. Sprinkle the 3 salts on top and serve.

SALT BOX

Haleakala Ruby Sea Salt, Molokai Red Sea Salt, Icelandic Lava Salt, Black Lava Salt, Black Diamond Flake Salt, Tsushima No Moshio, Shinkai Deep Sea Salt, San Juan Island Sea Salt

Homemade Ramen Noodles

MAKES 4 SERVINGS

The difference between ramen and other pasta is the addition of alkaline kansui (sodium carbonate). The pumped up alkalinity gives ramen their characteristic golden color and makes them super chewy. Kansui is available in powder and liquid form from your local Asian food market or online.

4 teaspoons kansui

1 teaspoon shio

⅔ cup hot water

2 cups all-purpose flour

Potato starch

SHIO BOX

Tsushima No Moshio, Shinkai
Deep Sea Salt, Jigen No Shio

Dissolve the kansui and shio in the hot water in a bowl.

Put the flour into the work bowl of a food processor fitted with a dough blade. With the machine running, slowly pour ½ cup of the liquid mixture into the feed tube until the flour is moistened and a dough starts to form. Stop the machine and scrape up any dry bits of flour from the bottom of the bowl into the moist dough that has formed. Turn the machine on again and add as much of the remaining liquid, a teaspoon at a time, as needed to form a smooth mass.

Knead in the food processor for 3 minutes, then remove from the work bowl and knead by hand for about 2 minutes.

Shape the dough into a square, wrap in plastic wrap, and refrigerate for 1 hour or up to overnight.

Divide the dough into 4 pieces and roll with a pasta machine using the same method as described in the fettuccine recipe (page 120). Stop rolling at setting 5.

Coat the noodles with potato starch to keep them from sticking. Use immediately, or wrap well and refrigerate for up to 3 days.

CHAPTER 7

SWEETS

I am not a big sweets eater, but put salt and sweet into competition, and I jump right from skipping dessert to having seconds. Sweets need something to bring out the underlying flavors, to give them some backbone. Salt doesn't just make sweets taste better, it also makes them taste worthwhile.

We taste lots of things with our tongues, and flavor scientists are constantly finding more and more taste receptors for specific flavors. At this point in history, we agree on five: sweet, salt, sour, bitter, and umami. One of the awesome things about these tastes is that once they exist in food they are always perceptible. One can never wipe out the perception of another. You've probably heard that if you oversalt something you can add sugar to diminish the saltiness. Not true. Sweet doesn't cancel salt, but it does counter it. Instead of neutralizing one another, sparks fly as the two tastes spar: sweet-salty, salty-sweet. Every time we try to pin our palates down to one, the other taste pops up. Salt and sweet are powerful competitors, but we can reap the benefits of both in every bite.

SALTS			pies	cookies	cakes	brownies	pastries	puddings	ice creams	confections
SWEETS										
fleur de sel			x	x	x	x	x	x	x	x
sel gris			x			x	x	x		x
flake	fine			x			x			x
	coarse		x	x	x	x	x	x	x	x
traditional	fine		x	x	x	x	x			
	coarse		x	x	x	x	x	x	x	x
shio										x
rock	fine		x	x	x	x	x			x
	coarse								x	x
	block		x	x	x				x	
infused	smoked		x	x	x	x	x	x	x	x
	flavored		x	x	x	x	x	x	x	x

Summary Berry Clafoutis with Fleur de Sel Brûlée

MAKES 6 SERVINGS

Drop your fear of pretentious French fare and go clafoutis. *Clafoutis* sounds to me like a combination of *doily* and *froufrou*, but they are in fact totally down to earth—among the most forgiving of French pastries. This dessert is sort of a cross between custard and pancakes, inundated with fruit. You literally can't screw it up. It has more fruit than most clafoutis, and the raspberries are especially juicy, so we've reduced the amount of milk from a traditional recipe. The finished cake-pie-crêpe-pudding is best served warm. We've added a pane of caramel on top, dusted with minute fleur de sel crystals.

Preheat the oven to 350°F. Spray the interior of a 9-inch round pan with oil.

Mix the flour, granulated sugar, and ¼ teaspoon of fleur de sel in a bowl. Whisk in the eggs, melted butter, and lime zest. Whisk in the milk until the batter is smooth and light. Fold in the blueberries and half the raspberries just until distributed evenly; do not overmix. Pour and scrape into the prepared cake pan. Top with the remaining half of the raspberries.

Bake until the clafoutis is set and golden, about 45 minutes. Cool on a rack for 20 minutes.

Sprinkle the turbinado sugar over the top of the clafoutis. Gently smooth the layer with the back of a spoon. There should be a thin, even layer across the surface, no more than a film. Too thick and the surface will burn before the sugar beneath melts and caramelizes.

Use a kitchen torch set to medium flame to melt and caramelize the sugar: Move the flame back and forth over the surface of the sugar (the tip of the flame should just touch the sugar) until all of the sugar is melted and browned. Immediately sprinkle the melted sugar with the remaining 1 teaspoon of fleur de sel before it sets.

Wait a few minutes for the sugar pane to set. Cut into wedges and serve.

Spray oil

½ cup all-purpose flour

½ cup granulated sugar

1¼ teaspoons fleur de sel, divided

3 large eggs

3 tablespoons unsalted butter, melted

Finely grated zest of 1 lime

¾ cup whole milk

1 pint fresh blueberries

1 pint fresh raspberries

3 tablespoons turbinado sugar

SALT BOX

Sal Rosada de Maras, Fiore di Cervia, Ilocano Asin, Sugpo Asin, Bitterman's Fleur de Sel, Gulf Coast White Sea Salt

Lavender Salted Lemon Blondies

MAKES 24 SERVINGS

Without salt these torte-like bar cookies are lemon goo through and through—delicious lemon goo, admittedly, but goo in search of higher meaning. Lavender salt, with its rich floral aroma and just-perceptible camphor edge, lends both logic and poetry to the lemon. Enticing texture, arousing aroma, and richer flavor, are all transformed by a few pinches into something you can believe in.

Spray oil

½ cup (1 stick) unsalted butter

1¼ cups ground unpeeled almonds

1 cup sugar

Finely grated zest and juice of 1 lemon

½ teaspoon vanilla extract

¼ teaspoon fleur de sel

1 extra-large egg

1 teaspoon baking powder

1 cup all-purpose flour

2 teaspoons Blue Lavender Flake Salt

Preheat the oven to 350°F. Coat an 8-inch square pan with spray oil.

In a large heavy saucepan over medium heat, melt the butter halfway. Add the almonds and continue cooking until the butter is completely melted, stirring constantly. Remove from the heat and stir in the sugar, lemon zest, lemon juice, vanilla, fleur de sel, and egg until smooth. Add the baking powder in pinches and stir until incorporated. Stir in the flour until there are no lumps. Scrape the batter into the prepared pan and spread into an even layer. Sprinkle the lavender salt over the top.

Bake for 20 minutes, or until lightly browned and just set. Cool on a rack for 30 minutes. Cut into 16 (2-inch) squares. Store in a tightly closed container at room temperature for up to 5 days. If storing longer, wrap individually and freeze for up to 2 months.

SALT BOX

Lavender salt is a great example of a strategic ingredient: It is more versatile and more effective than straight lavender. Use it in salads, crème brûlée, leg of lamb, goat cheese, and in honey over tart stone fruit.

Ugly Duckling Brownies with Chiles and Flake Salt

MAKES 16 SERVINGS

Intensely chocolate, exceptionally moist, dense without being heavy, these brownies camouflage themselves behind a humble crumbly exterior. If you have consumed anything chocolate sometime in the past decade, you are no doubt familiar with the sex appeal of chiles and chocolate. Chocolate and chile may be enjoying a love affair in this dessert, but crunchy shards of salt are what gives them wings.

Preheat the oven to 350°F. Coat a 9-inch square pan with spray oil.

In a large heavy saucepan over medium heat, melt the butter halfway. Add the chocolate and stir until the chocolate is half-melted. Add the chiles, remove from the heat, and stir until completely melted.

Add the sugar, cocoa, Fleur de Hell, and vanilla, and stir until smooth. Beat in the eggs until completely incorporated. Add the baking powder and stir to incorporate. Stir in the flour until there are no lumps.

Pour and scrape the batter into the prepared pan. Level the top and sprinkle with the flake salt. Bake until a tester inserted in the center comes out with a damp crumb clinging to it, 25 to 30 minutes. Do not overbake.

Cool completely in the pan on a rack overnight. Cut the pan into 16 brownies and lift out with a small spatula. To store them, stack in a tightly closed tin with parchment or plastic wrap between the layers, or wrap individually in plastic wrap and store for up to 5 days at room temperature; freeze for up to 1 month.

Spray oil

4 tablespoons (½ stick) unsalted butter

5 ounces semisweet chocolate, broken into pieces

1 teaspoon chopped ancho chiles

1 cup sugar

3 tablespoons cocoa powder

¼ teaspoon Fleur de Hell

1 teaspoon vanilla extract

3 large or extra-large eggs

1 teaspoon baking powder

⅓ cup all-purpose flour

1 teaspoon flake salt

SALT BOX

Brownies are fertile fields for playing with salt. You get a big bold crunch with French sel gris, an even bigger crunch with a coarse traditional salt, or try an infused salt like Taha'a Vanilla.

Devil's Food Layer Cake
with Salted Marshmallow Icing

MAKES 12 SERVINGS

It wasn't until I lived in France that I discovered that layer cake was more than a big spongy thing people ate at birthday parties. In Europe, cake is paned in glaze and sliced into discreet, pristine wedges barely thick enough to reach the rim of the plate. This is cake? Though hardly low-profile, this layer cake builds on the restrained audacity of European cake—tactile, firm, and bursting with flavor. Then it goes over the top by seasoning the devil's food with chocolate fleur de sel, studding the frosting with flaky vanilla salt, and speckling the top with more of the chocolate fleur de sel.

CAKE

Nonstick baking spray

¾ cup (1½ sticks) unsalted butter

4 ounces unsweetened chocolate

2½ cups packed dark brown sugar

2 teaspoons vanilla extract

1 teaspoon Chocolate Salt, plus more for garnish

4 large eggs

1½ teaspoons baking soda

2½ cups all-purpose flour

1 cup boiling water

ICING

1⅓ cups sugar

⅓ cup water

4 large egg whites

¼ teaspoon cream of tartar

1 teaspoon vanilla extract

1 tablespoon Taha'a Vanilla Salt

To make the cake, preheat the oven to 350°F. Grease and flour two (8-inch) cake pans with baking spray.

In a large heavy saucepan over medium heat, melt the butter until half melted. Stir in the chocolate. Remove from the heat and stir until everything is melted.

Stir in the sugar, vanilla, chocolate salt, and eggs. Add the baking soda in pinches, breaking up any lumps with your fingers. Stir thoroughly. Stir in the flour, just until well blended. Stir in the boiling water.

Pour into the prepared cake pans and bake for 25 to 30 minutes, until the cake is springy and pulls away slightly from the sides of the pan.

Cool on a rack for 5 minutes. Remove them from the pans, and let cool on a rack to room temperature, at least 2 hours.

To make the icing, mix the sugar and water in a medium heavy saucepan until the sugar is fully moistened. Cook over medium-high heat, stirring gently, until the sugar dissolves. When the syrup boils, stop stirring and let the syrup cook until it reaches 236°F on a candy thermometer, about 5 minutes.

Continued

SALT BOX

Any number of infused salts will
work wonderfully here, adding
a quiver of aroma to excite the
senses. No-brainers include Blue
Lavender Flake Salt, Lemon Flake
Salt, Orange Flake Salt, and
Pinot Noir Sea Salt.

Meanwhile, beat the egg whites and cream of tartar in a stand mixer fitted with the whisk attachment just until frothy. When the syrup is up to temperature, pour it in a thin stream into the whites, beating constantly on medium-high speed. Aim your stream of syrup just beside the rotating beaters. If some of the syrup should hit the beater, it will be thrown against the side of the bowl rather than into the egg whites, so try to avoid this (but it is going to happen some, so don't fret). Beat until the mixture is opaque, dense, and glossy, about 3 minutes. Add the vanilla and beat until the icing is barely warm, about another 3 minutes. Fold the vanilla salt into the meringue using a spatula.

To assemble, put one cake layer on a cake stand. Spread a thick layer of icing over the top. Top with the other layer. Spread the icing over the sides and finally over the top of the cake, swirling your icing spatula to create peaks across the top of the cake. Sprinkle with more chocolate salt. Cut in wedges to serve. Store any leftovers at room temperature, in a cake tin or loosely covered with plastic wrap, for up to 3 days.

Salt Chip Chocolate Chunk Cookies

MAKES 24 COOKIES

One bite of these cookies and your mind will vibrate with memories. On the way back from the beach in the family station wagon, my brother and I would wrestle madly. This was in the halcyon days before seatbelts, so we could fly over the back seat and land on the dog, jump back and land on each other, turn upside down or smash each other against a (often unlocked) door, oblivious to my harried parents yelling for us to stop it or they'd pull over. It's a wonder where caramelized brown sugar, dark chocolate chunks, and bright flakes of salt can take you. I've chosen black salt for these cookies because it looks like incognito chips, but white flake salt will work just as well.

Preheat the oven to 375°F. Line 2 baking sheets with parchment paper, aluminum foil, or silicone baking liners. (Do not grease.)

Mix the flour, baking soda, and fleur de sel in a small bowl.

Mix the butter and brown sugar in a large bowl of a stand mixer until creamy, scraping the sides of the bowl as needed. Beat in the vanilla and egg. Stir in the flour mixture until all of the dry ingredients are incorporated. Stir in the chocolate chunks with a spoon, and gently fold in the 1 teaspoon of black salt.

To form the cookies, scoop 24 (2-tablespoon, or 1-ounce) mounds onto a sheet of foil. Wet your hands and roll into balls. Equally space the balls of cookie dough on the baking sheets. You should get 12 cookies comfortably spaced per sheet. Wet your hands again and flatten the balls into ¼-inch-thick disks. Sprinkle the tops with the flake salt or more black salt.

Bake until browned on the bottom and edge, 9 minutes per batch. If you are baking both sheets at once, swap oven positions halfway through.

Cool the cookies on the sheet until set, about 5 minutes. Transfer with a small spatula to a wire rack to finish cooling. Store in a tightly closed container for up to 5 days at room temperature, or wrap tightly and freeze for up to 1 month.

1¼ cups all-purpose flour

½ teaspoon baking soda

¼ teaspoon fleur de sel

½ cup (1 stick) unsalted butter, softened

¾ cup packed light brown sugar

1¼ teaspoons vanilla extract

1 large egg

5 ounces semisweet chocolate, cut into ¼-inch chunks (makes 1 cup)

1 teaspoon black salt, plus more as needed

½ teaspoon coarse flake salt

SALT BOX

Black Salt: **Black Lava Salt, Icelandic Lava Salt**
White Flake Salt: **Cornish Flake Sea Salt, Maldon Sea Salt, Hana Flake Salt**

Apple Pie with Salted Walnut Streusel

MAKES 12 SERVINGS

My grandpa, a German immigrant who worked patriotically for the American cause during World War II as an engineer and inventor, would always amaze us with whatever tractor and garage door opener he had just manufactured by hand from his machine shop in the basement. What I also remember about him was that the man loved apple pie. The strangest thing about him, though, was his penchant for salting each bite. This Grandpa-ization of the all-American classic switches out the top crust for a salt-spangled avalanche of nutty streusel.

8 tablespoons (1 stick) unsalted butter, divided

3 pounds Granny Smith apples, peeled, cored, and thickly sliced

3 tablespoons fresh lemon juice

⅔ cup granulated sugar

Pinch of ground cloves

Pinch of ground nutmeg

2 teaspoons ground cinnamon, divided

2 tablespoons cornstarch

2 teaspoons vanilla extract

2 tablespoons rum

1 (9-inch) unbaked pie shell, store-bought or homemade

1½ cups chopped walnuts

¼ cup all-purpose flour

½ cup packed dark brown sugar

1 tablespoon sel gris or coarse traditional salt

Preheat the oven to 400°F.

Melt 4 tablespoons of the butter in a large skillet over medium heat. Cook the apples, lemon juice, sugar, cloves, nutmeg, and 1 teaspoon of the cinnamon until the apples are tender, about 10 minutes.

Remove from the heat and let cool, and then stir in the cornstarch, vanilla, and rum. Mound into the pie shell.

Mix the walnuts, flour, brown sugar, sel gris, remaining 1 teaspoon of cinnamon, and remaining 4 tablespoons of butter in a bowl, using your fingers, until the mixture is uniform and thoroughly crumbly. Pack into an even layer over the apples. Bake for 50 minutes to 1 hour, until the pastry and topping are brown and the filling is bubbling. Cool before slicing and serving.

SALT BOX

Piran Sel Gris, Dolce di Cervia, French sel gris, Popohaku Opal Sea Salt, Kona Deep Sea Salt, Maine Sea Salt, Wellfleet Sea Salt, North Fork Sea Salt, Oryx Desert Salt, J.Q. Dickinson

White Chocolate Bark with Dark Chocolate Salt

MAKES 6 TO 8 SERVINGS (ABOUT ¾ POUND)

White chocolate is supersweet stuff made from cocoa butter, milk, and sugar. Technically, it's not chocolate—at least according to some people. The white chocolate naysayers would tell you that cocoa solids contain all the chocolate flavor, not the cocoa butter, so white chocolate is just sweetened vegetable fat. It is true that white chocolate's lack of cocoa solids make it both cloyingly sweet and culinarily hard to classify. So is it really chocolate? If you're a glass-half-full person, consider that chocolate is naturally more than 50 percent cocoa butter. It's up to you to decide. Or better yet, embrace the argument, sprinkle it with chocolate salt, and let your senses battle it out.

Preheat the oven to 400°F.

Place the pecans on a sheet pan, and toast until browned and crisp, about 6 minutes, stirring once. Remove from the oven and let cool.

Put 6 ounces of the chocolate in a covered microwave-safe bowl and cook in the microwave at full power for 2 minutes, or in the top of a double boiler set over barely simmering water.

Meanwhile, chop the remaining 2 ounces of chocolate finely. Remove the melted chocolate from the microwave and mix with a whisk until smooth. Add the chopped chocolate in 2 or 3 handfuls, whisking in each addition before adding another. Stir in the nutmeg.

Fold the toasted pecans into the chocolate using a rubber spatula, folding until the nuts are completely coated and the chocolate begins to firm up. It is important that the chocolate is firm enough to mound around the nuts without being runny.

Pour and scrape the chocolate onto a sheet pan and spread into a rough rectangle about ½ inch thick. Sprinkle the top with the salt and allow to set completely at room temperature until hard, about 2 hours. When the chocolate is solid, cut into shards and serve. Store in a tightly closed tin at room temperature for up to 2 weeks.

1 cup unsalted pecan halves

8 ounces white chocolate, broken into pieces, divided

¼ teaspoon freshly grated nutmeg

2 teaspoons Chocolate Salt

SALT BOX

Equal parts Pinot Noir Sea Salt, Blue Lavender Flake Salt and Lemon Flake Salt, or Halen Môn Gold Sea Salt, Gulf Coast Pecan Smoked Salt, Persian Blue Salt, or try any other smoked salt, flavored salt, or rock salt.

Hot Mocha Sundaes with Sweet Salt Crunchies

MAKES 4 SERVINGS

The recipe on the box of rice cereal for marshmallow treats has to be the most lucrative recipe written. Enough rice cereal and marshmallows flow out the doors of supermarkets every day to float the Spanish Armada. Tragically, they got the recipe wrong. Here we load up the crispy treats with crunchy salt, and then break them apart to float on hot fudge sundaes. The salt-sweet-chocolate-crunch is a sensory deluge. If the cereal and marshmallow companies ever adopt this trick, I'm buying a boat.

3 tablespoons unsalted butter, divided

13 large marshmallows or ¾ cup mini marshmallows

2 cups crisp rice cereal

1 tablespoon sel gris, coarse traditional salt, or rock salt

⅔ cup natural cocoa powder (not Dutch-process)

¾ cup sugar

1 cup brewed coffee

¼ cup heavy cream

1 teaspoon vanilla extract

1 pint coffee ice cream or your choice of flavor

Melt 1 tablespoon of the butter in a medium saucepan over medium heat. Add the marshmallows and stir until completely melted. Stir in the rice cereal and salt until thoroughly combined. Pour onto a sheet pan and press in a thin layer. Cool completely, and then chop into fine pieces.

Mix the cocoa and sugar in a medium heavy saucepan. Slowly whisk in the coffee until smooth. Bring to a simmer, stirring frequently. Add the cream, and simmer for 3 minutes.

Add the remaining 2 tablespoons of butter, and simmer for 3 minutes more. Stir in the vanilla and let cool for 10 minutes.

Make sundaes with 2 scoops of ice cream, a dousing of warm mocha syrup, and a big handful of salty crunchies.

SALT BOX

Really want to dazzle? Serve your sundae in a luminous pink bowl cut from 600 million-year-old Himalayan salt. Make the recipe as directed, but omit the salt. An hour before you're ready to serve, place 4 small Himalayan salt bowls in the freezer. Take the chilled bowls out just before serving, then scoop in the ice cream and drizzle on the sauce. The longer the ice cream sits in the salt bowls, the more salty mineral flavor it will pick up.

CHAPTER 8

DRINKS AND COCKTAILS

Western cuisines make artificial distinctions between food and drink. Food is for nourishment, drink for refreshment. Food is cooked and drinks are blended. And most interestingly for our purposes here, there exists an erroneous assumption that food is salted and drinks are sweetened. This probably is why salting beverages feels radical. In many cultures, salt-forward drinks are popular. Take Vietnamese salted lemonade or Indian salted lassi. In India *jal-jeera*, a honey-sweetened lemonade with cumin and sulfuric Kala Namak, is a classic, and folks have been salting the wounds inflicted by tequila shots since the first gusano worm got soused. However, to the mainstream Western palate, drinking one's salt feels unnatural.

Similar to the salting of desserts, salting sweet beverages reinforces and complicates the sweetness. But it interacts with the other tastes as well. Salt buffers acids in fruit juice, wine, and beer. It mutes bitterness, bringing forward herbal and fruit flavors in tonics and hoppy beer. And it underscores savory notes in whiskey the same way it unleashes meaty flavors in steaks and chops.

There are four ways salt can be added to drinks:

1. Rimming: Applying salt crystals to the edge of a drinking glass adds dimension to the act of sipping. You experience both the texture and brininess of salt upfront, before the beverage ever passes your lips. When applying salt to a glass, moisten the outside of the rim and roll the wet area in a thin layer of salt spread out on a plate. Avoid salting the edge of the rim or the interior, to keep salt from falling into the drink.

2. Floating: Large flat crystals of flake salt will float on the surface of frothy drinks. Similar to rimming, floating salt crystals add textural impact, and because they don't dissolve easily, they play a secondary role as a surprising garnish.

3. Infusing: Sweet drinks, like drinking chocolate or sweetened coffee, develop deeper layers of flavor when salt is mixed directly into the beverage.

4. Perching: Perch a few flakes of salt on the peak of an ice rock jutting from the surface of a double Scotch. As the ice melts, it doesn't just release new aromas in the whisky through dilution; it also adds salinity, which underscores a Scotch's sweetness and grassy notes.

DRINKS AND COCKTAILS			rimming	floating	dissolving	perching
SALTS	fleur de sel		X		X	X
	sel gris					X
	flake	fine	X			X
		coarse	X	X		X
	traditional	fine	X		X	
		coarse	X			X
	shio		X		X	
	rock	fine	X		X	X
		coarse				
		block				
	infused	smoked	X	X		X
		flavored	X	X		X

Tamarind Margarita with Sumac Salt

MAKES 1 SERVING

Salting a margarita rim is more or less mandatory, but it fairly begs for a little innovation once in a while. Trying different salts is a great starting point. Another is to sail the drink in an entirely new direction by adding flavor to the salt. One of my favorite techniques is to add acidity to the salt, creating a tart salt sizzle that sets the drink ablaze. Tamarind and sumac are both exotic acidifiers. Tamarind is a tropical fruit that is only available outside its native Africa in concentrated paste or as dried fruit. The paste is easier to use, but it makes a darker margarita than a muddled tamarind pod. Sumac is a brick-red powder that is the ground dried fruit of a bush native to Iran. It has a tartness that's reminiscent of sucking on lemons, combining the sourness of lemon juice, the fragrance of lemon zest, and the bitterness of pith. In this riff on a classic margarita, tamarind takes the place of lime, and sumac tints and flavors the salt rim.

Mix the salt and sumac on a small plate. Moisten the outside of the rim of a double rocks or margarita glass with a bit of the agave syrup, and roll in the salt mixture.

Muddle the tamarind pod and lime in the bottom of a cocktail shaker. Add the remaining agave syrup, the tequila, and citrus liqueur. Put 1 (1-inch) ice cube in the glass and throw 3 more in the shaker, and shake until well chilled. Strain into the glass. Squeeze the lime wedge over the drink and drop it in; serve immediately.

¼ teaspoon Flor de Sal de Manzanillo

⅛ teaspoon ground dried sumac

½ ounce agave syrup, divided

1 dried tamarind pod, peeled

¼ lime

2 ounces blanco tequila

¾ ounce citrus liqueur, preferably lime

Lime wedge, for garnish

SALT BOX

In place of the sumac and salt, try Rosemary Flake Salt, Sage Salt, Fleur de Hell, Maldon Smoked Sea Salt, or Orange Flake Salt.

Salted Cardamom Drinking Chocolate

MAKES 6 SERVINGS

Hot cocoa is made with cocoa powder. Drinking chocolate is made with whole chocolate, meaning cocoa solids and cocoa butter both. It's the cocoa butter that makes whole chocolate that silky, melty heaven that it is, but because it is expensive, manufacturers steal it out from under your nose (and sell it back to you for use right under your nose . . . which is to say, they use it to make lipstick and balms). The silky richness of drinking chocolate is a perfect storm of goodness: It's tastier and richer, and because it requires less sugar and contains more natural chocolate, it's far, far healthier. In fact, it's flat-out healthy, so much so that there is serious medical research suggesting you should be drinking it every day. The last appeal of drinking chocolate is that it's a superb playground for salt, which excites the palate and shines light on every deliciously dark sip.

1 (13.66-ounce) can coconut milk, divided

3 cups water

¼ cup sugar

1 tablespoon cardamom seeds, cracked

½ cup cocoa (regular, not Dutch)

8 ounces bittersweet chocolate (at least 60% cacao), broken into pieces

6 pinches flake salt

Skim the cream from the top of the can of coconut milk. Add enough of the thin "milk" left in the can to make 1 cup. Set aside. Save the rest of the thin coconut milk for cooking or drinking.

Combine the water with the sugar and cardamom seeds in a medium saucepan. Bring to a boil, stirring occasionally. Boil for 1 minute. Remove from the heat and let steep for 5 minutes. Remove the cardamom seeds with a slotted spoon and stir in the cocoa. Return to a boil over medium heat, then remove from the heat. Add the chocolate and stir until melted. Add the reserved thinned coconut cream and froth with an immersion blender or in a blender.

Pour into warm mugs and top each with a pinch of salt.

SALT BOX

The challenge and the opportunity here is to find a salt that will land on the surface of your drink without sinking or dissolving. Soups, which are the college of choice for aspiring salters, are how I learned about the fine art of salting liquids, and they provide a great primer for exploring salted hot chocolate and drinking chocolate.

Halen Môn Silver Flake Sea Salt, Cyprus Silver Flake Sea Salt, Alaska Pure Sea Salt, Achill Island Sea Salt, Maldon Sea Salt, Cornish Flake Sea Salt, and Hana Flake Salt are good choices.

Salted Caramel Cold Brew Coffee

MAKES 2 SERVINGS (4 CUPS)

Cold brew coffee, made from ground beans steeped in room temperature water for about a day, is naturally sweeter and blander than coffee brewed conventionally: sweeter because less of the bitter alkaloids in the beans are extracted, and blander because it is lower in acid. A spark of acid is what makes coffee bright. Adding caramel to the mix brings back what's missing, but in a more delicious, caramelized way. And popping in some salt, especially aromatic Taha'a Vanilla, makes the caramel taste better, which makes the coffee taste better, which makes your day happier, which makes your life .00003422 percent happier, based on the assumption that you're going to live for 80 years. And if you don't, your percentage of happy days increases. So you can't lose.

1 cup sugar

3 cups water

1 tablespoon Taha'a Vanilla

¾ cup coarsely ground medium-roast coffee beans

Milk, for serving (optional)

SALT BOX

Takesumi Bamboo Sea Salt is a unique salt for coffee, even if you're a regular coffee salter. It's made by packing excellent craft salt into a hollow stalk of bamboo and incinerating it, then breaking away the charcoal exterior to reveal a flinty, carbonated salt. It does a remarkable job of balancing out and accentuating the natural flavors of coffee without diminishing anything.

Pour the sugar into a medium skillet, at least 1 inch deep. Put over medium-high heat and stir until the sugar melts and turn deep golden brown. At first it will look like nothing is happening, but after a few minutes some of the sugar will start to liquefy and become quite lumpy; keep stirring. When the last lumps have melted and the sugar looks like liquid mahogany, remove the pan from the heat and add the water. Stand back. The sugar will bubble and harden and loads of steam that can burn you will billow from the pan. When all the water is in the pan, start stirring again. Keep going until the caramel has all dissolved; the liquid does not need to return to a boil. Cool to room temperature.

Put the salt and ground coffee in a 32-ounce (1-quart) French press coffee pot. Add the cooled caramel water and stir to moisten all of the coffee grounds. Put the top on, but don't press down the plunger. Let stand at room temperature for 12 to 24 hours.

Press down the plunger and pour the cold pressed coffee into a glass of ice. Add milk, if you want.

Highland Spike with Smoky Scotch-Cured Cherry

MAKES 1 SERVING

This sophisticated riff on a Rusty Nail is all honey and smoke. Like a traditional RN, it is garnished with a cherry, but in this case the cherry is cured with peat-smoked salt and peat-stoked Laphroaig Scotch. Shimmering sheaves of Alaska Pure Alder Smoked Sea Salt shine through the amber pane of whisky. Due to the layered, pastry-like flakes of Halen Môn Gold Sea Salt, the crystals won't dissolve, retaining their form until you get ready to snare them on the cherry and spike them down your gullet.

Stir the Scotch and Drambuie over ice in a cocktail shaker or mixing glass until thoroughly chilled. Strain into a chilled cocktail glass and garnish with the cured cherry. Carefully drop the salt flakes on and around the cherry. Shake the bitters into a bar spoon and float on top of the drink. Serve immediately.

2 ounces single-malt Highland Scotch (I like GlenDronach)

1 ounce Drambuie

1 Smoky Scotch-Cured Cherry (recipe follows)

6 large flakes Alaska Pure Alder Smoked Sea Salt

5 dashes aromatic bitters (such as Boker's)

Smoky Scotch-Cured Cherries

MAKES 12 CHERRIES

12 jarred pitted cherries

1 ounce juice from jarred cherries

2 ounces peaty Scotch (preferably Laphroaig 10-year)

1 teaspoon peat-smoked salt or oak-smoked salt

Combine all of the ingredients in a small jar with a lid. Seal the jar; shake to dissolve the salt. Set aside for 24 hours. Refrigerate for up to 6 months.

SALT BOX

Vancouver Island Smoked Sea Salt, Bulls Bay Bourbon Barrel Smoked Flake, Maldon Smoked Sea Salt, Oryx Desert Smoked Salt, Icelandic Birch Smoked Sea Salt, Halen Môn Gold Sea Salt, J.Q. Dickinson

---

Michelada with Fleur de Hell Rim

MAKES 1 SERVING

There are lots of variations on this beertail, but ours exceeds on several fronts. First we rim the glass with Fleur de Hell, a proprietary salt blend made from pristine fleur de sel crystals blended with the superhot chile, bhut jolokia. Then we add aged tequila, which massively jumps the proof and therefore the flavor. And finally, we add way more condiments than anyone else we know. On the surface it might seem like a Frankencocktail that stitches together a michelada, a margarita, and a Bloody Mary, but it has such a bright and sunny disposition, you'll be glad for the company.

¼ teaspoon Fleur de Hell

1 lime wedge

2 ounces añejo tequila

1 ounce fresh lime juice

3 dashes hot pepper sauce

3 dashes aromatic bitters, such as Amargo Chuncho

3 dashes Worcestershire sauce

3 grindings black pepper

1 (12-ounce) bottle Mexican lager beer, chilled

Place the Fleur de Hell on a small plate. Moisten the outside rim of a pint glass with the lime wedge. Roll in the salt to rim the glass.

Put the tequila, lime juice, hot pepper sauce, bitters, Worcestershire, and pepper in a shaker. Fill with ice cubes and shake until cold, about 20 seconds. Strain into the prepared glass. Top with the beer. Garnish with the lime wedge, and drink up.

SALT BOX

Rather than talk about the kinds of salt that work well with this drink (just about any fleur de sel, a medium-fine traditional salt like Molokai Red Sea Salt, or a fine flake salt like Bitterman's Flake), let's talk about the other element of the salt rim: the liquid that moistens it. Moisten the rim with mezcal, or with orange bitters, or with elderflower syrup before rimming it with a beautiful salt. The mezcal will bring clean smokiness to the salt, the orange bitters will bring bright citrusy aroma, and the elderflower syrup will create a floral salty-sweetness that will stop you in your tracks.

Salty Dalmatian with B&W Ice Cubes

MAKES 1 SERVING

Vodka and grapefruit juice make a greyhound. Add an ice cube spotted with pepper and it becomes a dalmatian. Throw in a jigger of salty-sweet simple syrup and a salt-and-pepper rim and it's a Salty Dalmatian. Careful. He bites.

Mix the salt and pepper on a plate. Moisten the outside of the rim of a highball glass with a bit of the simple syrup and roll the moistened glass rim in the mixture.

Combine the vodka, remaining simple syrup, and grapefruit juice in a shaker filled with ice. Shake for 10 seconds, just until chilled; pour into the prepared glass. Plop go the ice cubes.

⅛ teaspoon flake salt

⅛ teaspoon coarsely ground black pepper

1 ounce Salted Simple Syrup (recipe follows), divided

2 ounces vodka

3 ounces fresh grapefruit juice

2 B&W Ice Cubes (page 150)

Salted Simple Syrup

MAKES 1½ CUPS

Place all of the ingredients in a small saucepan and stir to moisten the sugar. Bring to a boil over medium-high heat without stirring. Boil until clear, no more than 1 minute. Poor into a clean jar and cool. Refrigerate, tightly closed, for up to 2 months.

1 cup sugar

4 teaspoons sel gris

1 cup water

Continued

B&W Ice Cubes

MAKES 12 (1-INCH) ICE CUBES

1 cup crushed ice

1 teaspoon cracked black peppercorns

1 teaspoon cracked white peppercorns

1 cup cold water

Mix the crushed ice and peppercorns and divide between 12 partitions of a standard ice cube tray (about 1-inch square cubes). Add the cold water to fill each partition. Freeze until solid, about 2 hours.

CRAFT SALT

FIELD GUIDE

Salt is not just a seasoning; it's a tool for elevating your ingredients. Just as you need more than one kind of knife (paring and chef's knife) or pan (frying and saucepan), you need more than one kind of salt. There are seven basic kinds of salt: fleur de sel, sel gris, flake, traditional, shio, rock, and smoked/infused, plus special salts used exclusively for curing. The field guide that follows includes some of the more common and most useful salts available today. The more conversant you become with them, the more tools at your disposal for making the most of your food. The chart lists the salt families in order of importance. At a minimum, every kitchen needs these three: fleur de sel, sel gris, and flake salt.

NAME	ALTERNATE NAMES	STORY
■ = Fleur de Sel ▨ = Sel Gris ▨ = Flake ▨ = Traditional ■ = Shio ▨ = Rock ■ = Smoked ▨ = Infused ▢ = Curing		
Bitterman's Fleur de Sel	Guatemalan Fleur de Sel	A cross between a jungle, a farm, and a marine sanctuary, the salt farm provides vital ecological protection and economic opportunity in addition to supporting the education of underserved children in the community. Pacific seawater filters through a stunning mangrove forest, where it is evaporated under the hot harvest sun. The crystals are moist and gently crunchy, with a fresh but full-bodied mineral flavor. Pages 55, 74, 105, 129
Black Lava Salt	Bitterman's Black Lava	Guatemala's lush yet rugged volcanic landscape is mirrored in these panther-black crystals. Warm, mineral-rich fleur de sel crystals are carefully combined with detoxifying activated charcoal to create a visually stunning, mild but full-flavored salt. Pages 27, 33, 35, 59, 85, 88, 90, 105, 123, 135, 150
El Salvador Fleur de Sel	Mayan Sun	A classic French fleur de sel look and feel, but with a Central American twist. It has an incandescent warm white color; fine crystals with low moisture; and a friendly, silken salinity. Page 74
Fiore di Cervia		See also Dolce di Cervia. This fine-grained, brittle, translucent fleur de sel sparkles with the characteristic mineral sweetness of northern Adriatic salts. Pages 113, 129
Fiore di Galia		Trapani makes precious little fleur de sel. At Galia fleur de sel can be skimmed from across entire ponds thanks to the will, skill, and craft of the farmers. The result is a uniquely delicate, uniquely pristine fleur de sel with a mellow, mineral, almost fruity flavor. Pages 88, 113
Fiore di Trapani		Harvested from the northwest coast of Sicily, this salt comes from a single-estate salt farm in the city of Trapani. This area is a protected historic site from which salt has been harvested since the Phoenician era. Fleur de sel crystals are normally moist and crunchy, but these are coarser and more fiery tasting. Pages 25, 88, 113

NAME	ALTERNATE NAMES	STORY
■ = Fleur de Sel ▨ = Sel Gris ▨ = Flake ▨ = Traditional ■ = Shio ▨ = Rock ■ = Smoked ▨ = Infused □ = Curing		
Fleur de Sel de Camargue		On still mornings, sauniers, practiced salt farmers at Aigues-Mortes in the south of France rake fleur de sel crystals from the still surface of the salt pans before the wind disturbs the surface of the water. This is unusual because the vast majority of salt is made on an industrial scale, with heavy machinery. This hand-harvested salt is drier, finer, and more glitteringly transparent than many other fleurs de sel. Page 74
Fleur de Sel de l'Île de Noirmoutier	Fleur de Sel de Noirmoutier	From France's rugged Atlantic coast, this salt is known for its minute, highly irregular grains. It has a clean briny flavor like the ocean itself. It is among the finest of the French salts, with just enough moisture to lend gentle resiliency to every one of its myriad petite crystals. Pages 74, 88
Fleur de Sel de l'Île de Ré		Bicyclists and gourmands alike visit these salt fields in northwestern France. Oysters are grown in abundance, the wine is excellent, and the brandy is better (Cognac is nearby), but fleur de sel is the region's crown jewel. Impeccably fine crystals with a complex mineral flavor make it one of the world's best. Page 33
Fleur de Sel Guérande		The Celts first made salt here thousands of years ago. The flavor is slightly more mineral forward than the salts from neighboring Île de Ré and far wetter and slightly coarser than those of Camargue, from the south of France. See also Sel Gris de Guérande. Page 85
Flor de Sal de Manzanillo	Flor Blanca de Manzanillo	Evaporated under the blazing sun of western Mexico in salt farms up and down the coast of Manzanillo, only traditional methods are used here to harvest a spectacularly delicate, balanced, yet somehow vibrant fleur de sel. Pages 73, 88, 143
Flor de Sal do Algarve	Portuguese Flor de Sal	Due to the North African heat of Portugal's Algarve coast, fleur de sel crystals here form into a solid crust on the surface of the salt pans before they can sink. This crust is then raked off, yielding crystals that are large, almost fluffy, and distinctly fiery tasting. Pages 74, 105
Flos Salis		Made in the natural estuaries of the Atlantic coastline within the Ria Formosa and Castro Marim nature reserves of Portugal, crystals are allowed to grow for only a few hours before they are gathered. They are among the world's finest. This salt has a minute, fractured, scintillating, impeccable mineral balance. Pages 33, 74
Ilocano Asin	Pangasinan Star	The sea salt season in the Pangasinan region of the Philippines lasts six months, from the end of December to the end of May, when the rainy season resumes. Seawater is evaporated throughout the intensely hot day and then raked into baskets in the afternoon sun, yielding crystals that are an exaggerated version of fleur de sel. Lush, almost billowy, they goad the senses to explore beyond the safe boundaries, to use them boldly. Pages 85, 129
Piran Fleur de Sel	Piranske Soline Fior di Sale	This is the legendary Slovenian sea salt first documented in the 13th century, reaching its heyday as a centerpiece of the Venetian salt trade in the fifteenth to eighteenth centuries. It is the most blissful of fleurs de sel—a festive glitter of the finest confetti, with a unique, shimmering sweet flavor. Page 33
Sal Rosada de Maras	Peruvian Pink, Peruvian Warm Spring	Ten thousand feet up in the Peruvian Andes, a warm saline spring feeds an unlikely system of step-terraced salt ponds. Salt has been made here for two thousand years. The crystals glow a stunning pale flamingo pink color, and every gentle crunch delivers a rich, faintly sweet salinity. Page 129
Sugpo Asin		Sugpo Asin, which translates to tiger prawn salt, shines a pale pink color from the pink carotenoids produced by the shrimp that live in ponds that feed the salt works. Its crystals are large for a fleur de sel. The flavor is bright, rich, and agreeably aggressive. Pages 35, 105, 129
Piran Sel Gris		See also Piran Fleur de Sel. This salt takes a certain degree of spirituality and imagination to fully appreciate. The flavor is sweet and mild, yet the crystals are solid, almost hard—the shape and color of raindrops on a mirror. Pages 25, 32, 35, 53, 102, 113, 115, 136
Sal de Ibiza Granito	Granito de Ibiza	Granito ("small grain" in Spanish) is made exclusively using solar evaporation. These coarse, spangly, hard translucent crystals deliver a big wallop of fresh, slightly hot, faintly briny flavor. Pages 25, 53, 102

NAME	ALTERNATE NAMES	STORY
■ = Fleur de Sel	■ = Sel Gris	■ = Flake	■ = Traditional	■ = Shio	■ = Rock	■ = Smoked	■ = Infused	☐ = Curing

NAME	ALTERNATE NAMES	STORY
Sel Gris de Guérande	Celtic Salt, Gray Salt, Gros Sel, Bay Salt	At high tides, seawater from the swift Atlantic currents south of Brittany is collected, allowed to settle, and then channeled into the shallow salt fields dug in the porcelain clay. After the combined effect of sun and wind evaporates the seawater to a dense brine, it crystallizes to form crystal hunks with bold oceanic flavor. Trace amounts of silicates from the porcelain clay give the salt its characteristic color. Pages 25, 27, 32, 53, 55, 131, 136
Sel Gris de l'Île de Ré	Gray Salt, Gros Sel, Bay Salt	The west coast of France boasts one of the longest-lived salt-making traditions on earth. Paler than its cousins in Guérande and Île de Noirmoutier, the crystals are also milder, though still clearly expressive of the North Atlantic's briny soul. The salt has the same unctuous crunch as its brethren. Pages 25, 27, 32, 53, 88, 131, 136
Sel Gris de Noirmoutier	Bitterman's Sel Gris, Gray Salt, Gros Sel, Bay Salt	See also Fleur de Sel de l'Île de Noirmoutier. Cold, saline North Atlantic seawater is collected at high tide and allowed to settle in a silt pond before continuing its course to the shallow salt fields dug in the native clay. The sun and wind evaporates the seawater to a dense brine before it is flowed into salt pans to crystallize. This coarse, moist salt has the vibrant mineral flavor of a cold rainy day at sea and a surprisingly satisfying crunch. Pages 25, 27, 32, 55, 85, 131, 136
Achill Island Sea Salt	Achill Island Flake	The O'Malley family is reviving an industry that existed up until the 1820s on Keel Bay, Achill Island, in Ireland. Seawater is boiled over a gas fire in high-grade, stainless steel, open pan vessels, then the salt is dried in dehydrators. Pillow-fluffy flakes alternate between yielding and popping for a syncopated salinity bursting with briny effervescence. This salt is exceptionally high in minerals, and it shows, nicely. Pages 75, 95, 118, 145
Alaska Pure Sea Salt	Alaska Pure Flake	Jim and Darcy Michener make this salt in their back yard in Sitka, Alaska, from icy north Pacific seawater. Their first batches, back in 2007, were studies in the seasonal changes in ocean ecology, with spring, summer, winter, and fall, each tasting wildly different. Perfecting their process, the salt is now consistent in all the right ways: impossibly fragile crystals with impeccably balanced flavor. These are the first folks in North America to make a flake-style sea salt, and every crystal is proof of their mastery of the craft. Pages 40, 118, 145
Bitterman's Flake	Marlborough Flaky Sea Salt	This is a uniquely frothy, three-dimensional crystal unlike any other finishing salt on earth. It is harvested from the clear waters of the great southern oceans. Currents sweep up the east coast of New Zealand and into the solar salt field located right at the top of the South Island. These waters are evaporated using the natural processes of the sun and wind. This salt acquires its impossibly complex and light anhedral crystal structure by being very slowly evaporated in an open pan, allowing the formation of very light sea salt flakes. Pages 95, 96, 148
Black Diamond Flake Salt	Cyprus Black Lava Salt	See also Cyprus Silver Flake Sea Salt. Massive pyramidal crystals are darkened with detoxifying activated charcoal for big bold crunch from a dramatic black crystal. The flavor is very faintly tannic, which tames astringent foods like asparagus. Pages 27, 59, 90, 95, 105, 123, 150
Bulls Bay Carolina Flake		See also Bulls Bay Charleston Sea Salt. This flake variety boasts dry, medium-size bright white crystals with a big, bold flavor. Page 118
Cornish Flake Sea Salt	Cornish Flake	From Lizard Peninsula in Cornwall, England, seawater is filtered, concentrated into a saturated brine, then poured into vats, where it is gently heated until salt crystals gradually start to form on the surface. As the crystals grow, they sink to the bottom, where they are collected by hand. Flat, crispy crystals combine with jumbled wads and bits, creating faint savory seaweed flavors shining through assertive salinity. Pages 75, 99, 135, 145
Cyprus Silver Flake Sea Salt	Cyprus Flake, Falksalt	Hand-harvested by family-owned salt farms on the Mediterranean island of Cyprus, this solar-evaporated sea salt boasts distinctively enormous pyramidal crystals. Their structure is so sturdy that they don't crunch but explode, yielding a sharply pungent flavor. Pages 75, 99, 118, 145

NAME	ALTERNATE NAMES	STORY
■ = Fleur de Sel ■ = Sel Gris ■ = Flake ■ = Traditional ■ = Shio ■ = Rock ■ = Smoked □ = Infused □ = Curing		
Hakanai Flake		This Japanese sea salt is made by pre-evaporating seawater in greenhouses using traditional methods. The concentrated brine is then simmered at just the right temperature to create beautiful flakes of Hana Flake Salt (see page 155), but then, right before that happens, these ephemeral crystals form. Impossibly delicate crystals, more a glimpse of a flake than a true flake, impart superb mineral flavor. Pages 95, 96
Halen Môn Silver Flake Sea Salt	Halen Môn Pure White Sea Salt	Water from the frigid ocean currents of the Welsh coast is collected and simmered until complex, gemstonelike structures grow. And they keep growing, in layers, one upon another, until a stratified geometry forms, a filo dough crust of crunchy mineral brilliance. Pages 40, 75, 99, 118, 145
Hana Flake Salt	Hana No Shio	A miracle of Japanese salt-making craft, these icy white, semitranslucent crystals glimmer like moonlight in sunshine, and like sunshine in moonlight. The medium-size compressed pyramid-shaped crystals are unusual in how perfectly they hold together—until they are bitten. Then they pop and fragment and vanish as if they were never more than an illusion. The flavor is refined, silvery bitter sweetness. Pages 40, 75, 95, 99, 118, 135, 145
Havsnø Flaksalt	Havsnø	Michael and Arves Øverland use only renewable energy in their sea salt production and in their facilities and adhere to sustainable production practices. The process begins by first freezing the seawater to naturally concentrate the brine—an ancient method that was used in Norway in the 16th century. The crystals are a profusion of tiny, immaculate flakes with a texture and flavor as light as sea spray. Pages 40, 95, 96
Icelandic Flake Salt		From a small bay in the peninsula of Reykjanes, this is perhaps the world's only salt produced using only geothermal power. Seawater is evaporated using the heat from natural geysers, and all electricity used at the facility comes from a nearby geothermal power plant. The crystals are a fresh and clean-tasting tumult of nuggets and grains stacked into pinnacles and spires, an explosive landmass formed from the living sea and the Earth's ancient energy. Pages 40, 59
Icelandic Lava Salt		This salt is produced in a small bay in the peninsula of Reykjanes (an aspiring geopark applying for membership in the European Geopark Network). The salt is infused with activated charcoal. Rich dark color, crispy sparkly texture, and clear fresh flavor are its calling cards. Pages 27, 35, 85, 90, 105, 123, 135, 150
Jacobsen Flake		Seawater from Netarts Bay on the Oregon coast is boiled down over propane fire to make a concentrated brine that is then crystallized in open pans. Medium-size, diaphanous flakes pop to produce intense salinity. Page 75
Maldon Sea Salt		Naturally concentrated brine from England's Blackwater River estuary is evaporated in stainless steel salt pans mounted on an intricate system of brick flues fired by natural gas. This proprietary heating pattern gives birth to large yet parchment-fine pyramids and flakes that have become the salt maker's trademark. Their dazzling geometry snaps instantly into flickers and flashes of clean salinity. Salt has been produced in the area for millennia, and the saltworks stands on what is believed to be the site of a medieval saltworks. Pages 75, 99, 118, 135, 145
Murray River Salt	Murray Darling	This Australian salt gains its pale pink color from carotenoids produced by algae that live in the underground brine from which it is made. The color is matched with a cotton candy texture and a sweet note that imparts a sense of ineffable lightness. Page 95
Amagansett Sea Salt		Steven and Natalie Judelson pull seawater from the Atlantic Ocean off Amagansett, at the far eastern edge of Long Island, New York. Sun, wind, patience, and a strong back form the base of their recipe. Coarse, clunky crystals deliver the unbridled flavor of an angry Atlantic squall. Page 27
Antarctic Sea Salt		This salt is produced where the Antarctic Circumpolar Current brushes against South Africa. Clouded quartz color and minimal moisture pack big flavor into every massive coarse grain. Page 53

NAME	ALTERNATE NAMES	STORY
■ = Fleur de Sel ■ = Sel Gris ■ = Flake ■ = Traditional ■ = Shio ■ = Rock ■ = Smoked ▢ = Infused □ = Curing			

NAME	ALTERNATE NAMES	STORY
Bitterman's Fine Traditional Sea Salt	Fine Guatemalan Sea Salt	See also Bitterman's Fleur de Sel. This Guatemalan sea salt is ground to superfine, moderately dry crystals that distribute easily and dissolve instantly. The flavor is mild; with such mineral fullness it comes off as faintly buttery. Page 70
Bora Bora Sea Salt		Fabienne Bratschi captures the pristine seawater coursing past the small, impossibly remote island of Bora Bora in the South Pacific. The solar-evaporated and dried crystals are coarse, crumbly scree of flecks and ingots, but beautifully glistening, with a graceful, refined flavor. Page 64
Brazilian Sal Grosso	Brazilian Coarse	Harvested from the South Atlantic coast of Brazil, this coarse, translucent white traditional sea salt is made by the slow solar evaporation of seawater. Its rock-hard, wonky, melted meteorlike crystals are fresh tasting with a touch of hotness. Pages 29, 102
Bulls Bay Charleston Sea Salt		Rustin and Teresa Gooden began making salt on their South Carolina homestead in 2011. Drawing water at high tide from Bull's Bay, seawater is pumped into greenhouse evaporating pans, crystalized using solar and wind evaporation, then harvested by hand. The coarse, rubblelike crystals pack a hot, hard wallop. Page 64
Cuor di Trapani Sea Salt	Cuor di Sal di Trapani	See also Fiore di Galia. Coarse traditional sea salt from Galia is ground to fine crystals. Exceptionally rich in minerals, this salt dissolves instantly in a burst of rich, full flavor. Pages 56, 79, 86
Dolce di Cervia	Sale di Cervia	Il sale dolce, which translates as "sweet salt," is made in the lone remaining salt farm of the once great salt-making region of Cervia, just south of Ravenna, Italy. Solar-evaporated traditional sea salt is ground to a jumble of crystals and shards of all sizes, each with a faint harshness on the tongue that's accompanied by mild, mineral-sweet undertones. Pages 23, 25, 27, 32, 53, 88, 102, 113, 115, 119, 120, 136
Eggemoggin Reach Salt	Reach Salt	Born of a desire to return to Maine's rustic heritage, this salt is made by hauling buckets of seawater at the height of the coast's 11-foot tidal surge. The water is boiled down over a gas flame, then transferred to "baking trays" where low heat and constant stirring create a jumble of moist crystals with fierce flavor as wild as the coast itself. Page 78
Gulf Coast White Sea Salt		In Panama City, Florida, a strategic salt outpost during the Civil War, saltwater is first boiled down by 50 percent and then transferred to shallow pans to continue the evaporation process until all that remains are crumbly, puffy, soft chunks and rubble. The flavor is a strange, enticing combination of warm and savory. Page 129
Haleakala Ruby Sea Salt	Soul of the Sea Haleakala Red Sea Salt	Papohaku Opal (see page 157) is combined with sacred alaea volcanic clay to create a traditional Hawaiian salt with a deep, meaty red color. Hefty, invitingly supple crystals offer rich, refined flavor with an extraordinarily smooth, balanced finish—buttery and lush, outgoing and friendly. Pages 35, 85, 88, 123
J.Q. Dickinson	J.Q. Dickinson Heirloom Salt	Nancy Bruns and her brother, Lewis Payne, established their saltworks on the site of the family salt farm dating back to 1817. Where salt used to be made by pumping brine up from deep underground and boiling it off over fires, today it is put into sun houses where it evaporates and crystallizes. Firm, dry crystals deliver full, balanced saltiness with every satisfying crunch. Pages 48, 95, 115, 136, 147
Kilauea Onyx Sea Salt	Soul of the Sea Kilauea Black	In Kaunakakai, on the tiny island of Molokai, seawater is solar-evaporated to create an exceptionally mineral-rich salt (about 16 percent trace minerals) that is then combined with activated charcoal for color and to add detoxifying benefits. The thick, easily crunched crystals have a deep black color, a moist and silky texture, and a rich, almost buttery flavor. Pages 27, 35, 59, 85, 90, 105
Kona Deep Sea Salt	Kona Sea Salt	On the island of Hawaii, seawater from 2,200 feet below the surface slowly evaporates in a greenhouse to form crystals. The bluish and moist jumble of erratic nuggets and slivers crunch easily to reveal an exhilarating, mild, sweet flavor. Pages 25, 136
Maine Sea Salt	Maine Coast Sea Salt	Pioneers in the resurgent craft salt movement, Sharon and Steve Cook make this iconic salt by evaporating North Atlantic seawater in greenhouses. Its bold, intense, briny flavor and coarse, jagged crystals fill the mouth and the mind. Pages 53, 64, 78, 136

NAME	ALTERNATE NAMES	STORY
■ = Fleur de Sel ■ = Sel Gris ■ = Flake ■ = Traditional ■ = Shio ■ = Rock ■ = Smoked □ = Infused □ = Curing		
Molokai Red Sea Salt	Palm Island Premium Red Gold	Seawater sourced from the ultrapure waters around Molokai are solar-evaporated and combined with red alaea volcanic clay to achieve a mineral-rich sea salt with the clear, refreshing flavor of deep Pacific waters. The salt is used in Hawaii for both seasoning and preserving foods. Hawaiians believe that the baked alaea clay, which is composed of over 80 minerals, provides a variety of benefits including detoxifying and healing powers. It comes in both coarse and fine grinds. Pages 35, 85, 123, 148
Muối Biển	Traditional Vietnamese Sea Salt	This Vietnamese salt has terrifying, gargantuan, irregularly shaped pale cloud-gray crystals. Grown naturally using only solar evaporation, it is hand-harvested and often ground down to size before use with a mortar and pestle (often in the company of chiles, herbs, and spices). In its raw state, however, every daring crunch imparts a terrific explosion of salinity. Page 74
North Fork Sea Salt		Seawater off the coast of Long Island is collected by hand and evaporated over flame in open pans, carefully monitoring water temperature while salt crystals are in the blooming stage. The crystals are then scooped into a tray to be dried in the open air. The crystals crunch plushly, tossing out flavors that are at once sweet, harsh, briny, and slightly bitter—in an agreeable way. Pages 78, 136
Oryx Desert Salt		This salt is harvested in the Kalahari Desert. Saltwater is pumped from an underground salt lake sustained by underground rivers flowing over sedentary Dwyka rock strata dating from 250 to 300 million years ago. Huge, hard, pebbly, semiopaque crystals deliver vivid but restrained salinity. Page 136
Outer Banks Sea Salt		John and Amy Gaw were inspired by centuries-old traditions of salt making on the Outer Banks. North Atlantic seawater is collected in buckets and evaporated in large pots over fire to yield jumbled crystals that are then dried in an oven. The crystals remain moist and deliver vehement, in-your-face pungency. Page 78
Popohaku Opal Sea Salt	Soul of the Sea Papohaku White	In Kaunakakai, on the tiny island of Molokai, waters as pristine as any on the planet are solar-evaporated in mini greenhouses until crystals form. Packed with trace minerals (upwards of 16 percent), its rich, buttery flavor is peerless, complemented by a sumptuous opalescent white color, gregariously coarse crystals, and a pliant crunch that dissolves to a silky mouthfeel. Pages 79, 115, 136
Pure Sea Salt Co. Solar Sea Salt	Newfoundland Sea Salt	Bucking tradition, this salt is evaporated from seawater off the Newfoundland coast using only solar energy, rather than the wood fires used in the past. The crystals are a miniature rock slide of slivers and crags, with round flavor backed by a faintly tannic pungency. Page 48
Saltwest Naturals Sea Salt		The waters of the Pacific Northwest are among the world's lowest in ocean salinity. This salt is made by employing a reverse osmosis desalinization process, pumping water at high pressure through a set of semipermeable membranes to separate fresh water from seawater, creating potable water and concentrated brine that is evaporated over a fire. The crystals are superfine splinters and flecks with plenty of magnesium-rich moisture and a balanced mild but sparkly flavor. Pages 61, 101
San Juan Island Sea Salt		Brady Ryan offers one of the few examples of responsible salt making on the West Coast, evaporating filtered seawater in greenhouses, where the air reaches 135°F. The process takes between three to six weeks and captures abundant magnesium and potassium salts. The salt is dried using electric heaters, then ground to a medium-coarse jumble of splinters, spires, and nuggets with savage briny flavor that contrasts with its sunny, loving origins. Pages 55, 61, 70, 123
Sel Marin de Noirmoutier		Coarse, moist Sel Gris de Noirmoutier is ground up into superfine, silken, blue-grey crystals, making it easier to distribute evenly over food and quicker to dissolve. Grinding does nothing to mute the full, rich flavor of the original salt. Pages 79, 86, 101
Trapani e Marsala Sea Salt		Harvested in Sicily's sweltering summer heat, the "saline" (salt farms) of this region still follow salt-making traditions begun in Phoenician times. The salt, ground up into innocuous, cloud-white crystals, tastes hard and immovable, flat and impenetrable as the August sky. Pages 48, 56, 86, 113
Vancouver Island Sea Salt		Andrew Shepherd makes this salt by boiling seawater to a concentrated brine and then turning the heat way down (sometimes off) to allow the salt to separate from the water on its own. The superfine crystals have a pitched, full flavor. Pages 55, 70, 101

NAME	ALTERNATE NAMES	STORY
■ = Fleur de Sel ■ = Sel Gris ■ = Flake ■ = Traditional ■ = Shio ■ = Rock ■ = Smoked □ = Infused □ = Curing		
Wellfleet Sea Salt		In 1837 there were 658 saltworks on Cape Cod, producing 26,000 tons a year. A combination of railroads and ships delivering salt from less expensive locales, the advent of refrigeration, and other factors wiped it all out. Hope Schwartz-Leeper and Zachary Fagiano founded Wellfleet to revitalize the tradition of salt making in the area, pumping seawater into a large greenhouse about 300 gallons at a time. The crystals are a rubble of gravel and splinters and specks, contrasted with a distinctly sweet minerally flavor. Pages 64, 136
Yellowstone Natural Salt		Saline spring water in the Bridger-Teton National Forest is sealed in greenhouses and warmed gently by a geothermal hot spring. This unusual, carbon-free process yields firm, translucent crystals with clear, freshly sweet flavor followed by a tangy umami note. These are simple crystals packed with complex flavor. Pages 32, 64, 86, 101, 115
Aguni No Shio	Aguni Koshin Odo	On the remote Japanese island of Okinawa, hundreds of miles away from the big islands to the north, fresh seawater is filtered through bamboo branches, slowly evaporating it. The crystals made according to this ancient tradition are remarkably similar to a classic French fleur de sel, but with a hint of lovely bitterness peaking out behind a veil of fresh, clean flavor. Page 85
Amabito No Moshio		Moshio is the earliest known sea salt produced by the Japanese, dating back nearly 2,500 years. (Its name translates literally as "ancient sea salt.") It is made by evaporating brine with seaweed on the tiny island of Kami-Kamagari. A distinctively umami flavor lurks in its superfine café au lait–colored crystals. Pages 28, 55
Full Moon Shio		Made only in small batches, this Japanese salt follows the somewhat mystical tradition of harvesting seawater only during the evening of a full moon. This practice is said to maximize the mineral content and improve the flavor of the salt. Pages 56, 70, 79
Jigen No Moshio		Harvested in very small batches from the protected waters of a national park in Japan, this salt is slowly evaporated for eight days in a fire kiln to ensure a high mineral content. Fine, milk-white crystals surge with fierce yet balanced salinity. Pages 70, 79
Shinkai Deep Sea Salt	Suzu Shio	Shoji Koyachi brought back centuries-old salt-making traditions to Japan's Noto Peninsula, reanimating a craft that otherwise would be lost to time. Seawater from two thousand feet beneath the surface of the ocean is sprayed over bamboo mats suspended from the ceiling of a greenhouse. A week later, the resulting concentrated brine is boiled over a wood fire and then simmered until a mound of salt slowly emerges from the steaming cauldron. The resulting salt is 16 percent trace elements and moisture. Microfine fronds and flakes the color of glacial-core ice shimmer with an ecstatic bitter sweetness. Pages 55, 70, 79, 123, 124
Takesumi Bamboo Sea Salt		Icarus-like, this salt is hatched from bamboo segments that have been packed with Japanese deep sea salt and incinerated. The result is not so much a salt as a carbonated topping that, upon contact with the mouth, instantly dissolves into the sweetness of fizzled Pop Rocks. Pages 33, 146
Tsushima No Moshio		Although Japan is surrounded by seawater, the country's humid, rainy climate has never been well-suited for large-scale production of dry salt. It takes 10 tons of seaweed-infused water to make just 200 kilograms of the powder-fine, tawny-colored, savory salt. Pages 28, 54, 56, 70, 123, 124
Himalayan Pink Salt	Pink Himalayan, Pink Rock Salt	This rock salt is mined by hand from the purest seams of 500-million-year-old salt deposits deep under the rugged Punjabi landscape. (Contrary to popular belief, the mines are a good 200 miles south of the Himalayas.) The salt is pure and unadulterated, ranging from 97 to 99 percent sodium chloride, depending on which particular part of the deposit you test. The salt is mined in large boulders and then ground down to the desired coarseness. Hard pink crystals deliver assertive, almost spicy pungency. Pages 29, 56, 65, 87, 101, 102
Kala Namak	Black Salt, Sanchal, Bit Lobon, Kala Noon, Bire Noon	Widely used in Ayurvedic medicine for over two thousand years, this salt is made by heating rock salt to more than 140°F in clay pots and mixing it with Indian spices, including the seed of the black myrobalan tree called harad (part of triphala, an Ayurvedic herbal elixir). Kala Namak is used in the treatment of everything from weight loss to hysteria to good dental hygiene. As a rock, its color is deep purplish black; ground, it becomes pinkish brown; on your food, it takes on the hue of oxblood. It has the taste of savory-eggy sulfur dug from the belly of a slumbering volcano. Pages 48, 83, 104, 140

NAME	ALTERNATE NAMES	STORY
■ = Fleur de Sel ■ = Sel Gris ■ = Flake ■ = Traditional ■ = Shio ■ = Rock ■ = Smoked ☐ = Infused ☐ = Curing		
Persian Blue Salt	Prussian Blue Salt	From an ancient mine in Iran emerges one of the strangest feats of geological ingenuity: a pure, natural salt that's shot through with flecks and fields of dazzling peacock blue color. The pyrotechnic mystery of the color's origin (Is it trace amounts of metallic sodium? Is it an optical illusion created by irregularities in the crystal lattice? Is it neither? Both?) contrasts with the jovial elegance of its sweet, mild flavor. Pages 29, 56, 101, 102, 137
Redmond Real Salt	Red Rock Salt	An ancient sea once covered what is now much of North America, then retreated, and, eventually, evaporated, leaving the salt in undisturbed deposits in central Utah. Silts and volcanic ash sealed the salt, forming deposits that were eventually discovered by Native American Indians and finally were opened up to large-scale mining in the 1800s. The rock salt crystals are a speckle-work of translucencies, reds, and pinks. The flavor is big, brash, and as rugged as the West. Pages 29, 101, 102
Alaska Pure Alder Smoked Sea Salt	Alaska Alder Smoked	See also Alaska Pure Sea Salt. The Micheners cold-smoke their Alaska Pure Sea Salt flake salt with alderwood from their native Alaska. The crystals dissolve or crunch to release voluptuous, rich smoke that hovers somewhere in the olfactory hinterland between bacon and Fourth of July at the beach. Pages 38, 147
Bulls Bay Bourbon Barrel Smoked Flake		See also Bulls Bay Charleston Sea Salt. This smoked version gives off generous aromas of brown sugar, baking spices, and mild vanilla. Pages 27, 147
Danish Viking Smoked Salt	Danish Smoked Salt	Seawater from the Danish coast is boiled over fire until jumbled salt crystals form. These are then smoked with a variety of hardwoods, including cherry, beech, and juniper. The result is a bold campfire smokiness in dark, crunchy crystals. Page 38
Gulf Coast Pecan Smoked Salt		See also Gulf Coast White Sea Salt. The puffy white crystals are cold-smoked over pecan wood to a cozy golden brown. The aroma is rich and mapley with a pungent, woodsy flavor. Pages 115, 137
Halen Môn Gold Sea Salt	Pure Sea Salt Smoked Over Oak	See also Halen Môn Silver Flake Sea Salt. This salt is cold-smoked over oak to impart full-bodied smokiness. The golden nuggets of layered flakes boast an invitingly rich, gold color and vivid aromas of vanilla, oak, and campfires. Pages 27, 31, 137, 147
Icelandic Birch Smoked Sea Salt		See also Icelandic Flake Salt. This cold-smoked version brings gentle but still rustic aromas of a hearth fire. Page 147
Maine Apple Smoked Sea Salt		Coarse, mineral-rich Maine Sea Salt is painstakingly cold-smoked by hand over seasoned wood from apple trees. Coarse, intensely saline pebbles burst with intense bonfire aromas and traces of applewood sweetness. Page 27
Maine Hickory Smoked Sea Salt		See also Maine Apple Smoked Sea Salt. This version is cold-smoked with hickory wood, for nutty, slightly peppery, almost oily opulence. Page 114
Maldon Smoked Sea Salt		See also Maldon Sea Salt. This smoked version is cold-smoked with mixed hardwoods. The aromas are subtle, refined, with light astringency and sweetness. Pages 31, 48, 143, 147
Mesquite Smoked Sea Salt		See also Maine Apple Smoked Sea Salt. Cold-smoked with mesquite, these birdshot-size ochre crystals harbor aromas of a high plains fire pit the day after a buffalo hunt. Page 38
Oryx Desert Smoked Salt		See also Oryx Desert Salt. This version is cold-smoked with French oak. The crystals are hard, with mild aromas of diesel, peat, and oak. Pages 29, 53, 147
Red Alder Smoked Salt	Salish Alderwood Smoked Sea Salt	This pebble-textured Pacific sea salt brandishes intense aromas of alderwood smoke combined with the smoke of half a dozen other trees in the vicinity. The flavor is not unlike putting your tongue to an extinct campfire, and it kindles an urge to light it up and cook some more. Pages 31, 38, 48

NAME	ALTERNATE NAMES	STORY
■ = Fleur de Sel	■ = Sel Gris	■ = Flake ■ = Traditional ■ = Shio ■ = Rock ■ = Smoked ▨ = Infused ☐ = Curing
Sugar Maple Smoked Sea Salt		See also Maine Apple Smoked Sea Salt. This version offers plenty of smoke backed by gentle notes of spicy-sweetness. Pages 76, 115
Vancouver Island Smoked Sea Salt		Tawny-colored, fine crystals are cold-smoked over alder, apple, and maple woods for a mild bonfire aroma and a remarkably balanced, sweetly smoky flavor. Pages 27, 38, 147
Korean Bamboo Salt	Jukyeom, Amethyst Bamboo 9x Salt	Coarse sea salt is put into a canister of giant bamboo, capped with yellow clay, and baked. This ancient Korean process can be repeated, with the intensity of the eggy, umami flavor increasing each time. Bamboo 1x is baked once. 9x is baked nine times. 9x versions, called Jukyeom, are heated to 1,400 degrees and melted in the last step. Depending on the variety, colors can vary from amethyst to oyster, and pale beige to salt-and-pepper. The flavor ranges from mildly titillating to medievally punishing aromas of eggs cooked on a bed of lava. Pages 47, 49
Black Truffle Salt	Truffle	Sun-evaporated Sicilian sea salt is infused with Italian black summer truffles. The opulent aroma that pervades and fills the room with just a single sprinkle expands even bigger in the mouth, a potent, feral umami mushroominess that quickens the mind and swells the soul. Pages 100, 111, 113
Blue Lavender Flake Salt	Lavender Salt	Flake sea salt crystals are expertly infused with natural lavender and aroma. Lavender is a beautiful scent but can be tricky to use with food. Its heavy camphor notes can overwhelm or make food taste decidedly unfoodlike. Excellent lavender salt fixes this, delivering elegant floral notes that entwine effortlessly with sweet and savory flavors alike. Pages 40, 130, 134, 137
Cherry Plum Salt		This salt was inspired by a culinary institution in Japan, the umeboshi, or salt-preserved plum. Packing plums in a jar with sea salt pulls out 20 to 30 percent of the plum's liquid, which is used to infuse a fine shio. The superfine, pale pink crystals harbor a mild acidity that makes this salt unique. Page 55
Chocolate Salt		Guatemalan fleur de sel is blended with dark chocolate and natural chocolate flavor using a secret recipe. The medium-fine granular crystals are coffee colored, harboring moderate residual moisture and delivering decadent chocolaty flavor. Pages 16, 132, 134, 137
Fleur de Hell	Ghost Pepper Salt	Fleur de sel meets ghost pepper. One of the hottest peppers in the world, India's legendary bhut jolokia pepper is expertly infused into the glittering crystals of the salt world's natural-born leader, fleur de sel. Pages 14, 51, 60, 61, 74, 75, 131, 143, 148
Kamebishi Soy Salt		Shoyu (soy sauce) is fermented in one hundred-year-old cedar vats for three years. The resulting shoyu has 14.5 percent salt content by weight and is evaporated off to create dark chestnut-colored flakes and porous, pumicelike granules with rice-cake crunch and rich, purring umami flavor. Page 28
Lemon Flake Salt		Lemon Flake is hand-harvested from the Mediterranean Sea after being channeled through a network of dikes and ponds. Imposing pyramidal crystals provide an extraordinarily satisfying crunch, dappled with sunshine in the form of an infusion of bright, pungent, candy-sweet lemon juice flavor. Pages 74, 75, 134, 137
Orange Flake Salt		Fine flake sea salt is craftily infused with natural orange zest and aroma, yielding a salt with heady orange-forward fragrance and a sunshiny citrus grove taste. Pages 134, 143
Pesto Flake Salt		Parchment fine sea salt flakes are infused with DOP Genovese basil, authentic Parmigiano-Reggiano, earthy pine nuts, and aromatic garlic. Herbaceous, savory flakes transform in the mouth into liquid pesto. Pages 107, 112
Pinot Noir Sea Salt		Hand-harvested sea salt is infused with concentrated Pinot Noir wine. Vinous fragrance and magenta color dissolve into a tamarindlike tart sweetness that reverberates playfully against the salt. Pages 40, 75, 134, 137

NAME	ALTERNATE NAMES	STORY
■ = Fleur de Sel ■ = Sel Gris ■ = Flake ■ = Traditional ■ = Shio ■ = Rock ■ = Smoked ■ = Infused □ = Curing		
Rosemary Flake Salt		Hand-harvested flake sea salt is infused with fragrant rosemary. The fine shards and pyramids crackle to release the opulent perfumes of pine and fresh herbs. Pages 31, 40, 107, 143
Saffron Salt		Saffron is blended with fine-grained Sicilian sea salt to create something greater than the sum of its parts. Elegant yet pungent aromas burst with a complexity that cannot be defined in the grass, hay, grain, and honey notes that attempt to enclose it. No wonder saffron is the world's most expensive spice. This salt is the most cost-effective way to keep saffron in your diet. Pages 42, 43, 107
Sage Salt		Mineral-rich sea salt heads for the hills where it finds vibrant, heady sage. The crystals are a cacophony of flakes and jumbled grains that burst like a late summer herb garden in your mouth. Pages 31, 107, 143
Sal de Gusano		This traditional condiment from Oaxaca is made by combining Oaxaca sea salt with árbol and pasilla chiles and the dried larvae called gusanos. Gusanos feed on maguey roots, the plants grown to make mezcal, and are sometimes lurking at the bottom of the bottle—a macho and funny gift from the distiller. They are a delicacy in the region and lend crazy savory flavor to the spicy, zesty salt. Pages 28, 51, 69, 73, 74
Scorpion Salt		Hand-harvested fleur de sel from Guatemala is infused with the powdered moruga scorpion chile, one of the world's hottest chile peppers. The flavor is earthy and sweet beneath the merciless sting of chile heat. Pages 51, 61
Taha'a Vanilla	Halen Môn Pure Sea Salt with Vanilla	The seemingly simple combination of Tahitian vanilla pods and pure Halen Môn Silver Flake Sea Salt yields something that is anything but simple. Opulent vanilla aromas wake up the senses and the filo-flake crunch of minerally crystals whips them into a frenzy. The savory-sweet salt perfume is an untamable but delicious conundrum for the mind and for the mouth. Pages 74, 76, 89, 131, 132, 146
Prague Powder #1	Pink Salt, DQ Cure #1, Instacure #1, Curing Salt	Prague Powder #1 is a curing salt containing sodium chloride and sodium nitrate. The sodium nitrate helps with conversion of food proteins to preserve flavor and color and to provide better texture in cured meats. It is best for shorter cures. This salt is for curing only and must never be eaten straight as a seasoning. Pages 62, 63
Prague Powder #2	Instacure #2	Prague Powder #2 is a curing salt containing sodium chloride, sodium nitrate, and sodium nitrite. The sodium nitrate helps with conversion of food proteins to preserve flavor and color and to provide better texture in cured meats. It is best for longer cures. This salt is for curing only and must never be eaten straight as a seasoning. Page 63

Howard Bitterman, Pisa, Italy, 2015

ACKNOWLEDGMENTS

Writing books is the best way I know to study things I've always been curious about. Writing a book with Andy Schloss is the best way I know to study things I never even thought to be curious about. A lifelong seeker and a fearless creator, Andy is all any fellow could ask for in a collaborator or a friend. Kaitlin Hansen, my dear friend and passionate supporter, has made this book better not only with her discerning eye, but also by ruthlessly pushing me to be faithful to my ideas and ideals. I have the honor once again of singing the praises of my smart, supportive, and visionary editor, Jean Lucas. I think this book makes her the only editor in the world to produce two books on salt (not to mention one on bitters), and if that's not smart, supportive, and visionary, I don't know what is. Thanks to my art director, Tim Lynch, for manifesting and improving my wildest aesthetic dreams, time and time again. And thanks also to designer Holly Swayne for adding clarity and beauty to the hornet's nest of words, charts, and images that arrive in a heap on her desk, leaving in the form of this beautiful book. Thanks to Clare Barboza for the superb and generous photography and to Julie Hopper for her craftsmanship and artistry styling the recipes. My deepest thanks to my publisher, Kirsty Melville, who continues to believe in me and makes me feel like it all must be a dream. I couldn't have written this book without my fantastic teams at Bitterman Salt Co. and The Meadow—not only did they cover for me during my absences, they gave me inspiration to write in the first place. Thank you to my mother, Jill; my father, Howard; my sister, Jennifer; and my brothers, Aaron and Shem, for somehow sustaining an interest in my obsessions. I owe the biggest debt of all to my boys, Austin and Hugo, who must bear witness to the hellfire and damnation that rains down in our household whenever being a thoughtful and present dad takes a back seat to work. Last, thank you to all the makers of craft salt, for reviving the time-honored practices that once fueled the economies of the world and reinterpreting them in terms that bring nature, food, and community more intimately into our lives today.

METRIC CONVERSIONS AND EQUIVALENTS

APPROXIMATE METRIC EQUIVALENTS

Volume

¼ teaspoon	1 milliliter
½ teaspoon	2.5 milliliters
¾ teaspoon	4 milliliters
1 teaspoon	5 milliliters
1¼ teaspoons	6 milliliters
1½ teaspoons	7.5 milliliters
1¾ teaspoons	8.5 milliliters
2 teaspoons	10 milliliters
1 tablespoon (½ fluid ounce)	15 milliliters
2 tablespoons (1 fluid ounce)	30 milliliters
¼ cup	60 milliliters
⅓ cup	80 milliliters
½ cup (4 fluid ounces)	120 milliliters
⅔ cup	160 milliliters
¾ cup	180 milliliters
1 cup (8 fluid ounces)	240 milliliters
1¼ cups	300 milliliters
1½ cups (12 fluid ounces)	360 milliliters
1⅔ cups	400 milliliters
2 cups (1 pint)	460 milliliters
3 cups	700 milliliters
4 cups (1 quart)	0.95 liter
1 quart plus ¼ cup	1 liter
4 quarts (1 gallon)	3.8 liters

Weight

¼ ounce	7 grams
½ ounce	14 grams
¾ ounce	21 grams
1 ounce	28 grams
1¼ ounces	35 grams
1½ ounces	42.5 grams
1⅔ ounces	45 grams
2 ounces	57 grams
3 ounces	85 grams
4 ounces (¼ pound)	113 grams
5 ounces	142 grams
6 ounces	170 grams
7 ounces	198 grams
8 ounces (½ pound)	227 grams
16 ounces (1 pound)	454 grams
35.25 ounces (2.2 pounds)	1 kilogram

Length

⅛ inch	3 millimeters
¼ inch	6 millimeters
½ inch	1¼ centimeters
1 inch	2½ centimeters
2 inches	5 centimeters
2½ inches	6 centimeters
4 inches	10 centimeters
5 inches	13 centimeters
6 inches	15¼ centimeters
12 inches (1 foot)	30 centimeters

METRIC CONVERSION FORMULAS

To Convert	Multiply
Ounces to grams	Ounces by 28.35
Pounds to kilograms	Pounds by .454
Teaspoons to milliliters	Teaspoons by 4.93
Tablespoons to milliliters	Tablespoons by 14.79
Fluid ounces to milliliters	Fluid ounces by 29.57
Cups to milliliters	Cups by 236.59
Cups to liters	Cups by .236
Pints to liters	Pints by .473
Quarts to liters	Quarts by .946
Gallons to liters	Gallons by 3.785
Inches to centimeters	Inches by 2.54

OVEN TEMPERATURES

To convert Fahrenheit to Celsius, subtract 32 from Fahrenheit, multiply the result by 5, then divide by 9.

Description	Fahrenheit	Celsius	British Gas Mark
Very cool	200°	95°	0
Very cool	225°	110°	¼
Very cool	250°	120°	½
Cool	275°	135°	1
Cool	300°	150°	2
Warm	325°	165°	3
Moderate	350°	175°	4
Moderately hot	375°	190°	5
Fairly hot	400°	200°	6
Hot	425°	220°	7
Very hot	450°	230°	8
Very hot	475°	245°	9

COMMON INGREDIENTS AND THEIR APPROXIMATE EQUIVALENTS

1 cup uncooked white rice = 185 grams
1 cup all-purpose flour = 125 grams
1 stick butter (4 ounces • ½ cup • 8 tablespoons) = 115 grams
1 cup butter (8 ounces • 2 sticks • 16 tablespoons) = 225 grams
1 cup brown sugar, firmly packed = 220 grams
1 cup granulated sugar = 200 grams

Information compiled from a variety of sources, including *Recipes into Type* by Joan Whitman and Dolores Simon (Newton, MA: Biscuit Books, 1993); *The New Food Lover's Companion* by Sharon Tyler Herbst (Hauppauge, NY: Barron's, 2013); and *Rosemary Brown's Big Kitchen Instruction Book* (Kansas City, MO: Andrews McMeel, 1998).

INDEX

Andrews McMeel Publishing
a division of Andrews McMeel Universal
1130 Walnut Street, Kansas City, Missouri 64106

www.andrewsmcmeel.com

16 17 18 19 20 SDB 10 9 8 7 6 5 4 3 2 1

ISBN: 978-1-4494-7805-6

Library of Congress Control Number: 2016936621

Editor: Jean Z. Lucas
Designer: Holly Swayne
Creative Director: Tim Lynch
Production Editor: Maureen Sullivan
Production Manager: Carol Coe
Food Stylist: Julie Hopper
Photo credits: Mark Bitterman, pages ii, vi, 3, 15, 16, 17,
    22, 49, 57, 68, 82, 94, 110, 128, 142, 162